USING

SCENARIOS

A Publication in the Berrett-Koehler
Organizational Performance Series
Richard A. Swanson and Barbara L. Swanson, series editors

USING
SCENARIOS

Scenario Planning for Improving Organizations

Thomas J. Chermack

Berrett–Koehler Publishers, Inc.

Berrett-Koehler Publishers, Inc.
1333 Broadway, Suite 1000
Oakland, CA 94612-1921
Tel: (510) 817-2277
Fax: (510) 817-2278
www.bkconnection.com

ORDERING INFORMATION
Quantity sales. Special discounts are available on quantity purchases by corporations, associations, and others. For details, contact the "Special Sales Department" at the Berrett-Koehler address above.
Individual sales. Berrett-Koehler publications are available through most bookstores. They can also be ordered directly from Berrett-Koehler:
Tel: (800) 929-2929; Fax: (802) 864-7626; www.bkconnection.com.
Orders for college textbook / course adoption use.
Please contact Berrett-Koehler: Tel: (800) 929-2929; Fax: (802) 864-7626.

Distributed to the U.S. trade and internationally by Penguin Random House Publisher Services.

Berrett-Koehler and the BK logo are registered trademarks of Berrett-Koehler Publishers, Inc.

Printed in the United States of America

Berrett-Koehler books are printed on long-lasting acid-free paper. When it is available, we choose paper that has been manufactured by environmentally responsible processes. These may include using trees grown in sustainable forests, incorporating recycled paper, minimizing chlorine in bleaching, or recycling the energy produced at the paper mill.

Library of Congress Cataloging-in-Publication Data

Names: Chermack, Thomas J., author.
Title: Using scenarios : scenario planning for improving organizations / Thomas J. Chermack.
Description: First edition. | Oakland, CA : Berrett-Koehler Publishers, Inc., [2022] | Series: A publication in the Berrett-Koehler organizational performance series | Includes bibliographical references and index.
Identifiers: LCCN 2021034190 (print) | LCCN 2021034191 (ebook) | ISBN 9781523092888 (paperback) | ISBN 9781523092895 (adobe pdf) | ISBN 9781523092901 (epub)
Subjects: LCSH: Management—Simulation methods. | Strategic planning—Simulation methods.
Classification: LCC HD30.26 .C58 2022 (print) | LCC HD30.26 (ebook) | DDC 658.4/012—dc23/eng/20211015
LC record available at https://lccn.loc.gov/2021034190
LC ebook record available at https://lccn.loc.gov/2021034191

First Edition

28 27 26 25 24 23 22   10 9 8 7 6 5 4 3 2 1

Book producer: Westchester Publishing Services
Cover designer: Nola Burger

For Isla—The Light of My Life!

Contents

PART ONE. Exploring the Use of Scenarios

PART TWO. Specific Ways to Use Scenarios

PART THREE. Improving Organizations with Scenarios

Figures

The fundamental premise of *Using Scenarios* is that having scenarios doesn't mean anything if you don't know how to use them. Creating scenarios is an important step in understanding how the external environment could change. It is a necessary activity, but it is not sufficient. In order to understand the benefits of scenarios, you have to be able to use them. This is a book about how to do that. Many approaches to scenario planning result in a few scenarios that may be provocative and help people think differently about the future. Although this can be a stimulating activity, it usually falls far short of what scenarios can really accomplish.

The scenario planning literature is dominated by various methods for creating scenarios. The existing approaches include anywhere from 6 to 18 steps, and some avoid steps entirely. Regardless of the specific approach used to create scenarios, there is no standard advice for how to apply scenarios. While some methods do mention the idea of using scenarios, none offer detailed guidance on how to apply and use scenarios in a practical way. Even though the term "scenario" is more popular than ever, few people or organizations really understand what it means to develop scenarios and how to use them to support organizational change. As scenario practices have become more popular, the need for clear guidance on how to use them has never been more important.

Much of the available scenario guidance remains in the conceptual realm. But scenario planning is an applied activity. This mismatch creates a clear need for practical advice and detailed tools. This is an applied book. Its contents are intended to help you actively connect scenarios to action. Many diverse examples are provided, but there is no single, complete case drawn through all of the tools. The reason for this was to show a variety of examples and to illustrate that the approaches have been developed to be context and industry neutral. The processes, exercises, and workshops described have been used in organizations across industries and countries for over 10 years. They are effective. Because of the practical and specific nature of this book, it does assume a degree of familiarity with scenario planning. It is intended for those who have some experience in the field and want to consider ways to get more out of their scenarios. The material requires some basic fluency with scenario terminology and existing processes. However, significant effort went into making these tools easy to use for any scenario, strategy, organization development, or change management professional. If you have never worked on a set of scenarios, you may want to start there; or you could work with a mentor who can walk you through the whole scenario planning process.

Overview of the Contents

Using Scenarios is based on the premise that to truly add value with scenarios, going beyond simply creating them is required. To support this assertion, *Using Scenarios* is organized in three sections: Part 1: "Exploring the Use of Scenarios"; Part 2: "Specific Ways to Use Scenarios"; and Part 3: "Improving Organizations with Scenarios." "Exploring the Use of Scenarios" describes the need for this book in detail, as well as the problems with the practices of strategic and scenario planning. This section also describes the most common methods for developing scenarios. The review of current scenario planning methods is not intended to be comprehensive; rather, it is meant to give a general idea of the different ways to build scenarios and the general methods available. "Specific Ways to Use Scenarios," the core of the book, describes seven specific ways to use scenarios once you have built them. Scenario purposes, generating strategies, testing strategies, windtunneling, decision analysis, financial benefits, financial models, and signals are the focus. The chapters in this section provide examples, detailed guidance, and workshop instructions intended to help you actually apply the tools. "Improving Organizations with Scenarios" tackles the issue of how to make scenarios a standard part of organizational culture. Further, recommendations for advancing strategic and scenario planning overall are made.

Initially, these tools may seem complicated. Some are more complex than others, but all of them can be learned and applied by anyone seeking to get more out of scenarios than just enjoyable stories. As with most things, the more you use these tools, the better you will get at using them. The opportunity to connect scenarios to strategy and action can have many benefits: the ability to react quickly, the ability to anticipate major changes in the environment, decision-making support, and identifying major opportunities, all of which have potential financial returns that can be estimated. The output of using the tools and approaches described here will serve to demonstrate effective scenario planning that far exceeds its costs.

PART ONE

EXPLORING THE USE OF SCENARIOS

1 ▪ What Do You Do with Scenarios?

The fundamental purpose of this book is to provide practical guidance on how to use and apply scenarios for improving organizations.

Introduction and the Problem

What do you do with scenarios? The common product of scenario planning is a set of alternative futures. The lack of clear guidance on what to do with scenarios results in an incomplete process. It also leaves decision makers unsatisfied with the results because they cannot see the benefit. Existing scenario planning methods cover the various approaches for creating, developing, and writing scenarios but neglect approaches for how to use them. This book fills that void by describing different and precise ways of actually using scenarios. There is currently a serious lack of detailed guidance on the possible uses of scenarios, their intended outcomes, their benefits, and exactly how to facilitate scenarios as a change management process. *Using Scenarios* is intended to fill a very important need in the scenario and strategy fields by focusing on the use and implementation of scenarios.

Scenario planners often say that one-third of the time should be spent creating scenarios and two-thirds of the time should be spent using them. Yet, the available guidance focuses almost entirely on different ways to create scenarios. There is little, if any, guidance on how to use them. To be fair, some of the available resources do refer to ways of using scenarios but do not provide enough detail to show you how to do it. Precisely how that two-thirds of the time should be spent is vague and impossible to apply.

To deal with fast-changing environments, most organizations rely on strategy. Strategy and strategic planning have a mixed performance record, often relying on old tools that produce vague and nonactionable outcomes. Strategy and scenario planning professionals are often in a difficult position because the tools they use generally do not deliver the expected results. It is obvious that uncertain environments are difficult to navigate, and most people agree that it is impossible to predict the future. In practice, however, it is easy to fall back on the assumption that the future can be predicted when what CEOs, executives, and managers want most is steady organizational growth and returns to shareholders. Stability remains the unstated, unreachable goal. The problem, then, has two parts:

1. There is no practical guidance on what to do with scenarios once you have them.
2. The lack of using scenarios has prevented widespread adoption of scenario planning and integration with strategy.

The potential role for scenarios has exploded owing to increasingly uncertain business environments. There is now more interest in scenarios than ever. The COVID-19 pandemic was a serious turning point for attention to scenario planning, and the result is an opportunity.

The Opportunity

Organizations need help. With interest in scenarios at an all-time high, there is a real opportunity to demonstrate their value, integrate them with strategy, and adopt them more widely. This requires going beyond interesting stories. Detailed guidance for using scenarios is needed.

The solution should be obvious. To solve the problem and its two parts, scenarios need to be used, and they need to be integrated with strategy. This book presents seven approaches for applying and implementing scenarios for different outcomes:

1. Connecting scenarios to a purpose
2. Generating strategies
3. Creating and stress-testing strategic plans with scenarios
4. Testing decisions and options with scenarios
5. Assessing the financial benefits of scenarios
6. Modeling financials with scenarios
7. Developing scenario signals and critical uncertainty dashboards

Using Scenarios gives you the details you need to put scenarios into practice. Based on extensive experience and research, it is highly practical, and the logic is that if scenarios are put to use, they stand a much better chance of becoming a standard organizational planning activity. Corporate decision making is often very shortsighted, and with the tools provided in this book, you will be able to help leaders make more careful, thoughtful, and long-term decisions.

The content is intended as a follow-on to my previous work on scenario planning, *Scenario Planning in Organizations*, although it could easily be "bolted" onto any other scenario building method. It does not matter which method you have used to create scenarios.

The goal of this book is to advance scenario planning practice through detailed descriptions of seven different ways of using scenarios. Each is designed for achieving specific purposes and outcomes. Scenario planning has been slow to evolve, and one reason for the lack of development is a failure to explicitly show how to put scenarios into action. This book provides the necessary details and tools to improve current scenario planning practices. Exercise descriptions, templates, workshop structures, and guidance on how to apply the seven approaches are included.

If we continue to ignore the importance of what happens after a set of scenarios is created, we do nothing more than present interesting stories. Interesting stories do not support decision making or allow decision makers to consider the risks and benefits of potential actions. Interesting stories do not convince decision makers of the value of an investment or allow them to analyze the potential outcomes of substantial investments. If we continue to ignore the importance of showing how to use scenarios, the risk is a lost opportunity, a stagnated practice, and a discipline that does not advance.

Summary

This chapter has described the need for *Using Scenarios* and explained its major premises. Scenario planners have choices for how to go about improving organizations and how to most effectively deliver their work. Instead of understanding the fundamental need to link scenarios to strategy work, many scenario planners have been satisfied with delivering a set of plausible scenarios. No matter how good they may be, scenarios will not have an impact unless they are connected to decision making and, ultimately, results. In most organizations, strategic work that doesn't have an impact is dismissed and certainly not adopted. Demonstrating the value of scenarios and going beyond thinking tools are critical to advancing the field and improving organizations.

2 ■ Problems with the Practice of Strategic Planning and Scenario Planning

How many times have you heard the following?

- "We don't want our strategy to be another dust-collecting report that sits on the shelf!"
- "We want our strategic plan to become a living document!"
- "The scenario planning work was very interesting, but we really can't do anything with it."
- "Scenario planning helped us to think creatively, but we can't connect that creative effect to action, or any kind of financial impact."

These reactions might evoke a smile because you've heard them so many times before. The smile quickly fades when you are faced with the reality that these common outcomes of strategic and scenario planning are precisely what leaders don't want to happen. For the majority of organizations, a planning document that sits on the shelf, collects dust, and is not alive is usually the case. And scenarios often do not go beyond being viewed as interesting descriptions of possible futures.

Strategy and scenarios are necessarily linked. Ideally, scenarios open up thinking, and strategy gets to action decisions. Each realm of practice is missing something: scenarios lack a connection to action, and strategy lacks up-front analysis of multiple futures. Though some have tried, simply pushing the two processes together misses the mark. Taking a closer look at how these two processes can be more effectively connected is critical for getting to better organizational futures. This book provides a stepping-stone between scenario planning and strategic planning—it is an effort intended to address the gap between them.

One challenge put forth in this book is that scenarios are critical to strategy, and the connection between the two is essential for advancement. The way to accomplish this connection is to describe how scenarios can be used, which is the purpose of this book. When thinking about how to advance the practice of scenario and strategic planning, keep these definitions in mind:

- *Scenarios* are descriptions of multiple, different futures.
- *Scenario planning* is the process of developing scenarios *and* using them for strategic action.
- *Strategy* is how an organization intends to reach its goals and objectives.
- *Strategic planning* is the process of developing goals and objectives *and* describing how to achieve them.

Strategy and scenarios can have great utility, though there are problems with the practice of both. Understanding the common reasons why strategic and scenario planning often fail is the first step toward improved practice. Because these processes address how organizations fit in their environments, improving how these processes are practiced is an important and serious objective.

Strategic planning has a long history of mixed results (Iyanda Ismail et al., 2020; Kanu, 2020; Nilsson et al., 2020; Rudd et al., 2008). It is often something done on an annual basis because it has always been done. Why do companies conduct strategic planning each year? Maybe because it is comfortable, people know what to expect, and it can often be concluded in about two days? In most cases it's like the required reading for the year ahead. It is simply going through the motions—easy and predictable. The ritual carries on, even though most people are aware that it does not produce the desired living strategy. Finally, the majority of strategic plans contain such general and vaguely defined strategies that you couldn't possibly do a single thing with them!

Take, for example, the following strategic plan (this is an actual strategic plan from a real organization):

- Become the premier conference in [our discipline]
- Multimodal technologies
- Leadership structure
- Nonprofit status
- New member recruitment
- Electronic journal
- New website
- Strategic planning
- Working groups structure
- Sponsorships and partnerships
- Multicultural networking

There is not enough context for you to make a true assessment of this plan, though no amount of context can get around the fact that these are simply ideas. To be fair, the "plan" did contain a few paragraphs describing each of these ideas but offered no measurement strategies, scope, schedule, budget, or goals—nothing specific. The elements of this strategic plan are so vague they are impossible to implement. A listing of ideas does not make for an effective strategic plan, and you are probably all too familiar with strategic plans that look like this. How can "strategic planning" be part of the strategic plan?

Although I start this chapter rather critically, I do want to note that a lot of excellent strategy work is being done, many organizations are able to implement their strategic plans elegantly, and plenty of organizations are doing important strategy work that allows them to disrupt their industries. These are the market leaders, the companies that truly innovate and those that have developed ways of using various strategy tools to understand what might be coming. It is also easy to cherry-pick examples of strategy success (e.g., Apple, Amazon, or JPMorgan Chase). The fact is that while there may be examples of great companies that exercise discipline in their strategy work, the vast majority do not. As a result, strategy can be described as folly: persisting in a course of action with the understanding that it will not achieve the desired results or could make things worse (Schaefer & Guenther, 2016).

The purpose of this chapter is to describe the common problems in the practice of strategic and scenario planning. An extensive literature covers these problems, and it is not the goal here to provide a comprehensive and detailed review. However, major works are described in order to give a sense of the status of each realm of practice.

Problems with the Practice of Strategic Planning

Problems with the practice of strategic planning are well documented (Mintzberg, 1994a; Nickols, 2016; Wolf & Floyd, 2017). Perhaps the most leveling critique is Mintzberg's *The Rise and Fall of Strategic Planning* (2000). Warren's *The Trouble with Strategy* (2012) is not any more kind. Yet, arguably little, if anything, has changed. There is no need for a comprehensive review of the strategy research—it remains conflicting and inconclusive (Miller & Cardinal, 1994; Pearce et al., 1987; Wright et al., 2005). However, it is useful to review two aggressive critiques of strategy because they are comprehensive and summarize the status of the discipline and all of its debates.

The Fall and Rise of Strategic Planning

Mintzberg has been a giant within the strategy literature over the past 40 years. His contributions have certainly shaped the field. While critical at times, his scholarship has been firmly grounded in practice, recognizing the applied nature of strategy work. His seminal work on the status of strategic planning first appeared in

1994 in a *Harvard Business Review* article titled "The Fall and Rise of Strategic Planning." His critique identified several foundational problems with the practice of strategic planning, and it is clear there has been little to no response to the claims he made over 20 years ago.

The Fallacy of Prediction

A fundamental assumption in strategy is that the world stays still while planning happens. "How in the world can any company know the period for which it can forecast with a given accuracy?" (Mintzberg, 1994a, p. 110). There are so many historical examples of exactly why the idea that the future can be predicted is false, it is hardly worth mentioning again. However, it is important for this chapter because this very fallacy is what led Pierre Wack and others at Shell Oil to develop scenario planning as a potential solution. We have to face the fact that we cannot predict the future and never will be able to. Mintzberg made it clear that "the forecasting of discontinuities, such as a technological innovation or a price increase, is virtually impossible" (1994a, p. 110). Can we close the book on this? The recent situation with COVID-19 should make it clear—you cannot predict the future!

Even though more and more sophisticated models of forecasting emerge each year, they are built on one single thing: data. Because it is "data," executives tend to believe that anything called data represents hard facts (Nalborczyk, 2020; Obar, 2015; see also Anderson, 1994; Austin, 1994; Ocasio & Joseph, 2008; Zeleny, 1997). Taking a closer look at the data and understanding where it comes from can reveal important insights. Most data come from databases that compile various measurements across an industry. It is incorrect, however, to assume that these data compare similar examples across companies. Another incorrect assumption is that available data are relevant to your organization. Most often, what these databases contain are recommendations based on correlations across the subscribing companies (Warren, 2012).

The dangers of correlation versus causation are also well documented (Norris, 2019), and the difference between the two can be easily summarized. I'm sure you can recall sitting on an airplane when the "fasten seatbelt" light was turned on. What usually follows is the shaking of the airplane. Based on the observed evidence alone, one could easily conclude that the illuminated light caused the airplane to shake. In reality, there was a complicated set of events that happened before the plane started shaking: the pilot received a report that turbulence was ahead, the pilot switched on the seatbelt sign, and then the airplane entered the environment of instability that caused the airplane to shake. Apply this metaphor to your organization just for a moment. How many times have leaders and managers mistaken correlation for causation? Probably many more than you think.

While this may be a simplistic example, the results in the organizational world do not differ greatly. Perceptions often inform action, and perceptions are not often connected to analysis, understanding, or evidence. The point is that many large stashes of "data" include reports from a variety of companies, of various sizes, in various industries. It is a serious mistake to understand the correlations among the data as causation. To be specific, a database may show a correlation between profitability and market share for a given industry. Let's say the reported correlation in the database is 0.58 (a zero correlation would mean that none of the relationship can be explained, while a 1.00 correlation would indicate that all of the relationship can be explained). A 0.58 correlation statistic suggests you have a nearly 50/50 chance! Buyer beware—understand where your "data" come from, how relevant they actually are to your organization, and how to interpret the correlation statistics.

The Fallacy of Detachment

"Strategic planning is to the executive suite what Taylor's work-study methods were to the factory floor—a way to circumvent human idiosyncrasies in order to systematize behavior" (Mintzberg, 1994a, p. 110). In this view, a goal of strategic planning is for senior managers to be provided with lots of "hard data" so that they can make decisions and formulate strategies to be rolled out and sent to those below to "do." These senior managers do the thinking, and the doing is left to those lower down in the organization. The separation of strategy into thinking and doing is a false dichotomy according to

Mintzberg, and he recognized that "work processes must be fully understood before they can be formally programmed" (1994b, p. 110). It is also possible that they cannot be programmed at all.

There are many stories of executives who actually have no idea about the details of the work that is carried out further down in the organization (Capon, 1996; Hendry, 2002; Toney & Brown, 1997). Indeed, it is troublesome how many senior managers and executives are entirely divorced from the skill required, processes needed, and collaboration necessary to deliver their products to customers. One remedy for this is for senior managers and executives to spend a day or two with a direct report. What impact would that have?

The Fallacy of Formalization

"Formal systems, mechanical or otherwise, have offered no improved means of dealing with the information overload of human brains; indeed, they have often made matters worse. All the promises about artificial intelligence, expert systems, and the link improving if not replacing human intuition never materialized at the strategy level" (Mintzberg, 1994b, p. 111). It is clear that artificial intelligence has come a long way since 1994, when Mintzberg wrote his critique. However, the critique is still valid. There are not yet instances of machine learning and artificial intelligence that can replace strategy and guide an organization's future. Despite the advances, we have not yet been able to fully replace human creativity with algorithms. You may cite Facebook (Caplan & Boyd, 2018) or the fact that machines can now create novel works of art (Elgammal, 2019) and music (Dredge, 2019), yet we are a long way from replacing the human ingenuity required for strategy work, where ideas come from, industry analysis, development of strategic options, understanding of where and when to take them, under what circumstances and—perhaps most important—whether to initiate them at all.

For all the promises of artificial intelligence and machine learning, there is little evidence that the human spirit of purpose, sustainability, and thinking about future generations, among so many other uniquely human characteristics, can be built into computer programming. We are not yet at a time when computers can think, act, react, reframe, and redesign anywhere near the abilities of the human brain and thinking process. Sure, computers can process data far faster and generate numerous possible outcomes—and they are overwhelming to the human decision maker trying to set a strategic agenda for the organization.

Deliberate versus Emergent Strategy

Mintzberg has been clear in differentiating between deliberate and emergent strategy (Mintzberg, 2004; Mintzberg et al., 2020; Mintzberg & Waters, 1985; see also Bodwell & Chermack, 2010). By his own admission, it is a somewhat misleading premise. No strategy is entirely deliberate, and no strategy is entirely emergent. "As implied earlier, few, if any, strategies are purely deliberate, just as few are purely emergent. One means no learning, the other means no control. All real-world strategies need to mix these in some way" (Mintzberg, 2004, p. 11; see also Mintzberg et al., 2020). The art of combining these two properties of strategy is not clear, though the point is clear: there has to be some flexibility involved in strategy making.

Summary

Mintzberg has been highly critical of the strategy industry, where it came from, and how it was formed. He has specific ideas about how strategy should and should not be developed. His later book *Strategy Safari* (Mintzberg et al., 2020) described 10 different schools of strategy in an effort to comprehensively summarize the evolution of strategy as a discipline. It is a useful tour of strategy, and it recognizes the high degree of ambiguity involved in any strategy work.

Warren's *The Trouble with Strategy*

Warren's (2012) review began with summaries of the good, the bad, and the ugly when it comes to strategy. His critique was far more specific than Mintzberg's. For the good, Warren described companies such as Nucor, Kimberly-Clark, and Pitney-Bowes as organizations that were able to achieve a significant turnaround and sustain recovered high performance for many years. Skype, Zipcar, Netflix, and Amazon were other examples. "Note that good strategy is not all about the market-facing end of the business; it also needs solid choices and effective implementation in the engine room that develops, produces, and supplies a company's products or services" (Warren, 2012, p. 10). On the bad side, Warren cited British Airways and KLM's attempts to compete in the low-fare market. These were cases of poor decisions to compete in new markets that neither airline could actually execute; they simply couldn't match the low prices of competitors Ryanair and easyJet. They went ahead with it anyway. "The error lies in persisting with the effort when there is no evidence of its working" (Warren, 2012, p. 14). Acquisitions were another target. "Studies over many decades have found that most acquisitions destroy value for the acquiring firm, but this does not stem the steady stream of badly mistaken acquisitions" (Warren, 2012, p. 15). Finally, obsession with next quarter's results, rather than a long-term view, was described as another critical reason for strategy failure. Looking at the 2008 recession, Warren described how the Rabobank Group (one of the Netherlands' largest financial entities) was one of very few organizations that stockpiled about 30 billion euro in preparation for the potential collapse it saw downstream.

Drawing from research by Kaplan and Norton (2001), Warren reported:

> Strategy is patchy at best. One of many investigations reported the following:
>
> - 75% of executive teams did not have a clear customer proposition.
> - Less than 5% of a typical organization's workforce understood the organization's strategy.
> - Only 51% of senior managers, 21% of middle managers and 7% of line employees had personal goals linked to their organization's strategy.
> - Up to 25% of strategy measures changed each year.
> (2012, p. 46)

Warren's (2012) critique focused on four core problems with the practice of strategic planning: (1) emulating successful organizations, (2) situating strategy in the finance team, (3) misusing strategy tools, and (4) improperly educating strategy professionals.

Emulating Successful Organizations

It can be tempting to find an example of success and try to emulate it. This practice invades strategy in the same way it does leadership. Trying to emulate a rock star performer—whether a person or an organization—is a guaranteed disappointment. Consider the many biographies of how to lead like Jack Welch or Steve Jobs. Sure, observing great performance can have lessons, and that performance has to be scrutinized before it is blindly adopted and applied. A key winning strategy that worked for Amazon in the digital marketplace will not necessarily work for an organization in the manufacturing sector or the retail industry. It has been too tempting to simply try to replicate a successful strategy used by a given organization, thinking, "it will work for me too."

"There is a common tendency in strategy writing to look for success stories and then hold those cases up as infallible role models for all to follow" (Warren, 2012, p. 8). The dangers that come from this practice are extreme. Just like "data," it is impossible to substitute what another organization might have done for what your organization should do. It is a custom world. As markets become more and more segmented, sliced up, and separated, the keen observer will understand that analysis is perhaps the last remaining tool. Yes, there are numerous strategy "tools," and each could make a contribution, depending on the commitment of the people involved. The ability to discern what a given organization has done and what parts of that might be relevant for your organization requires being a student of your organization and the industry.

Situating Strategy in the Finance Team

Since the 1990s, strategy has been absorbed into the finance team. A recent study by McKinsey showed that the strategy function was based in finance in 956 Fortune 1000 companies (Miles & Poppe,

2017). Warren observed that finance has an important function in organizational operations, "but they don't understand strategy" (2012, p. 40). In describing the finance approach to strategy, Warren documented the following steps: (1) prepare and analyze historical financials, (2) build the revenue forecast, (3) forecast the income statement, and (4) forecast the balance sheet. Without attention to the external environment, competitor analysis, market opportunities, and resources available, how can this be called strategy? Developing insights, deeply understanding the market, and becoming aware of significant potential shifts require thinking outside of financial ratios and internal cash flows.

The 1990s were the glory days of strategy professionals. Then, companies were stocked with bright young people, equipped with everything they learned in their MBA programs and ready to deploy significant resources toward strategic management (Micklethwait & Wooldridge, 1996). There were strategy departments. Yes, these were the golden years for strategy professionals, and they had the resources to deliver across the board. At the time, there were entire units dedicated to the science of strategic management, and most large companies had extensive expertise at their disposal. So what went wrong? The research literature shows that those large strategy teams and departments could not return the investment they required (Micklethwait & Wooldridge, 1996). Today, numerous consulting companies advocate for "strategic finance," which eerily follows almost the same steps Warren described almost 10 years ago.

Strategy Tools

Strategy tools have always been—and will continue to be—a serious mystery:

> In 2010, strategy consultants McKinsey & Company concluded a two-year study entitled the Strategy Theory Initiative. This was a fundamental and thorough review of all the academic literature in the field, along with all the consultants' tools they could find, and was intended to identify the really powerful theories and methods. After two years of work by a team of

some of their brightest and most experienced consultants, they found virtually nothing. (Warren, 2012, p. 81)

The most common tools used in strategic planning remain those that have been used for decades: SWOT analysis, market segmentation, value-chain analysis, competitor analysis, 5-forces, 7-S's, and on down the line. While each of these can be useful, none is adequate on its own. Sometimes the list includes scenario planning, and on closer examination what is usually produced is nothing more than best-case, worst-case, and status quo scenarios (Warren, 2012). Hardly how scenarios were intended to be used (more on this to come). The point is that the tools most often used are haphazard and reflect the disdain for the quantitative preferences of every MBA-trained CEO.

SWOT Analysis

At the top of the list is SWOT analysis (figure 2.1), which deserves special attention. This simple matrix of considering an organization's strengths, weaknesses, opportunities, and threats is the basis of most strategy work today. Why?

Not to repeat more thorough critiques elsewhere, but the shortcomings of this tool are dismissed again and again. Yet it remains probably the most commonly used strategy tool. There is no question that there can be value in studying an organization's strengths,

	Strengths	Weaknesses
Opportunities	Achieve opportunities that greatly match the organizational strengths	Overcome weaknesses to attain opportunities
Threats	Use strengths to reduce the organization's vulnerability to threats	Prevent weaknesses to avoid making the organization more susceptible to threats

Figure 2.1. SWOT Analysis

weaknesses, opportunities, and threats. What is usually produced is a long list of bullet points that are all far too vague to be useful. "Superior customer service" and "dominant market share" are common strength bullets. "Grow market share" and "acquire a firm" are common opportunities. Weaknesses are not often acknowledged, and threats are usually dismissed or downplayed at best. The SWOT exercise can be characterized as a chance to support existing beliefs in the organization's superiority and, without attention to the external environment, to downplay the risks and threats. A useful SWOT analysis has to have some grounding in evidence and information about the external environment, which is usually absent. It should be clear that as generally practiced, the SWOT analysis is not sufficient as the sole strategy tool. Yet, it is used that way consistently.

SWOT analyses often lead to checklists and lists of options. Lists are good, and someone has to ask the question of what they are based on. If they are based only on the perceptions of managers and executives, they are worth little. The key to a useful SWOT analysis is to have evidence, or some kind of market data, survey, or interview research, to build into each quadrant.

2 × 2 Boxes

Warren developed a clear criticism against 2 × 2 grids as a whole. Specifically citing the growth share matrix (figure 2.2) of the Boston Consulting Group (BCG), Warren took it apart.

The BCG growth share matrix has "relative market share" on the x axis. On the y axis is the growth rate (in % per year). This matrix creates (obviously) four quadrants. They have been famously named "Stars" (upper left), "Cash cows" (lower left), "Dogs" (lower right), and "??" (upper right). The BCG matrix has caused more controversy over the past few decades than any other strategy tool. To be fair, it was never intended as a sole solution to organizational strategy, yet some leaders have taken it as just that.

In fact, the misuse of the BCG matrix ultimately led many corporations to diversify and buy other businesses that had nothing to do with their core purposes, in order to show representation in each

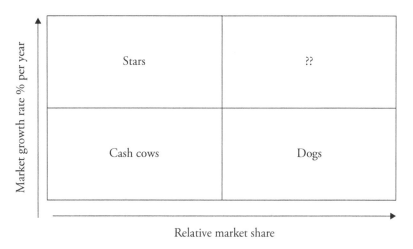

Figure 2.2. BCG Matrix

quadrant (Warren, 2012). In the 1970s and 1980s many of these corporations were broken apart and sold off as the realization that their overall worth was less than the smaller companies came to light.

Ratios and Benchmarking

The widespread involvement of academics and research firms trying to understand and compare performance has led to a reliance on statistics and ratios (Warren, 2012). A host of consultants specializing in the development of various databases that allow you to compare your firm's performance with that of others has become a go-to strategy tool for many. The rise of six sigma and statistical business process control underscores the appeal of this kind of analytic management of strategy. To echo Mintzberg—be warned—these tools can appear elegant, rigorous, and highly quantitative, but all too often the comparisons do not involve enough similarity to be useful. For example, Warren cited an oil production organization in the North Sea: "A detailed study by a leading consulting firm for one of the major operators concluded that it was grossly overspending on maintenance compared with its most efficient competitors. The firm cut its spending and implemented tight procedures and controls. . . . Five years later, the equipment involved was in a dire condition, often breaking down, interrupting production, costing millions of dollars to fix and even compromising safety" (2012, p. 65).

Frameworks and Diagrams

Every management consulting company has its own set of frameworks and diagrams that it uses to guide its practice. Usually, these are decks of PowerPoint files that each consultant is taught to deliver. Most also sell them to their clients. While it is sometimes useful to create an image of a complex process, most frameworks and diagrams are really lists dressed up with boxes and arrows. Sometimes these boxes are arranged in a way that intends to demonstrate causation (e.g., competitive advantage causes performance), but these attempts create more problems than they solve (Warren, 2012). "First, yet again, the words [in the boxes] are abstract and vague. We already explained that the field can't even define competitive advantage or performance and this fluff continues: what exactly is a Resource and how is it different from a Capability? . . . Secondly, even if we agree on definitions, we hit another problem: it isn't clear how to *measure* what we are talking about" (Warren, 2012, p. 69).

Useful Tools

Warren cited four strategy tools as having stood the test of time and having actual utility: (1) the Experience Curve, (2) Porter's Five Forces, (3) the value curve, and (4) scenario planning. The Experience Curve was developed by the Boston Consulting Group in the 1960s. "This method explains how unit costs of novel manufactured products fall as a company's cumulative production (its experience) grows" (Warren, 2012, p. 73). More of a heuristic or rule of thumb than a strategy tool, the Experience Curve provides a way to understand expected performance as an organization grows. Porter's Five Forces were first published in 1980. The tool provides five factors to consider when thinking about the competitive environment for any organization. "The fact is that there is a perfectly sound five-forces story to tell about the emergence of industries as diverse as low-fare airlines, cell phones, flat-screen TV's and even web browsers and so-cial networks" (Warren, 2012, p. 74). The value curve illustrates that focusing on what customers value and what they might be willing to make a value "trade-off" for can reveal new business models or op-portunities. Using the example of a low-cost airline, Warren argued that customers are willing to "trade off" certain benefits or perks for a cheap ticket price. Finally, Warren did mention the use of scenario planning as a genuinely effective way of building uncertainty into the planning process. The caveat was that they have to be more than simple best-case, worst-case and status quo scenarios.

It is important to acknowledge that while highly critical of the field of strategy in general, Warren did highlight the important take-aways and the thinking tools that have actually been useful. His analysis could certainly be contested, though it is difficult to find an organization today whose leaders are truly satisfied with their stra-tegic planning processes. If you can find one, most will tell you that much of what they do is a certain kind of "corporate rain dance" and they try something new each year with fingers crossed, yet ultimately rely on the standard tools we have just reviewed (Micklethwait & Wooldridge, 1996).

Strategy Education

Most people who have some responsibility for strategy have learned what they know in MBA programs. Throughout the 1980s and 1990s, the degree was considered essential for consultants and managers. MBA curricula are governed by the Association to Advance Colle-giate Schools of Business (AACSB). The purpose of this accrediting body is to ensure consistency across schools of business in what they teach. As a result, what is approved to be taught is difficult to change. There have been serious criticisms of MBA programs over the years (Mintzberg, 2004), and some have even announced the degree is dead (Cross et al., 2020). As of late 2020 (according to the AACSB), the standard MBA curriculum includes courses in marketing, fi-nance, accounting, leadership, economics, and accountability and ethics. Nothing here is related to strategy, unless you consider finance and economics the basis of strategy.

Particularly related to strategy, the standard MBA curriculum usually includes only a single course on the topic (Warren, 2012), which is usually optional. Given the latest content areas promoted by the AACSB (above), it should be obvious that strategy, strategic planning, and other related processes are buried elsewhere. It should be easy to see why this is problematic. Setting this issue aside, Warren went straight to the bigger issue of *who* teaches strategy:

> Try this. If you are currently taking a strategy course, whether in an MBA programme or an executive course, ask your professor if they have ever actually developed a strategy for a real organization, lived with it for years, and adapted it as competitive conditions changed and the organization itself developed. If the answer is no, ask in what technical strategy methods they do have expertise and whether they will teach you that expertise. Then ask what other technical skills are needed to do strategy properly and who will be teaching you those. (Warren, 2012, p. 117)

MBA and executive strategy courses have largely become content training courses; they teach you *about* strategy, not how to do it. They are not applied. This leads to one of Warren's key conclusions: many of those responsible for strategy have been taught by professors who have never done it, and in a learning experience that does not require application. The famous (or infamous) Harvard Case Study Method has also convinced thousands of emerging strategy professionals that they can read a 20-page case and know what to do (Servant-Miklos, 2019). While the case study method can be useful, it is usually misleading at best, providing a false confidence in strategic decision making.

Solutions and Summary

Warren was harsh in his assessment of strategic planning, though he was careful to call out the exceptions to his criticism where appropriate. The main problems have been outlined in order to demonstrate that strategic planning rarely delivers results. Yet, again, the annual corporate rain dance occurs with astonishing regularity and usually involves a jaw-dropping price tag.

Warren offered not only a critique but also a straightforward set of suggestions for improving the situation. He started with senior management. He recommended asking the following questions:

- Do you *really* understand your organization's strategy and how it is evolving as market and competitive conditions develop?
- Do you *really* have a rigorous quantitative understanding of how changes in the main parts of your business interact to drive your performance?
- Do you *really* understand the nature and scale of change in your markets and channels?
- Do you have any *real* idea what your competitors are up to, what impact their actions will have on your performance over time, and precisely what you should be doing about it? (2012, p. 143)

Second, Warren suggested placing a strategy professional on each business team. The intent is not to revive the large strategy teams and departments of the 1990s but rather to stratify strategy expertise across the organization. Obvious departments might include HR, marketing, information systems, and finance, among many others. The point is to distribute strategy as a system within the larger organizational system.

Next was the issue of consultants. "Strategy consultants themselves face a dilemma. On the one hand, they will likely get better work, and see it implemented—and implemented better—if clients have some clue as to why it all makes sense. On the other hand, if clued-in clients stop accepting proposals for pointless projects, the consultants may not get engagements at all" (Warren, 2012, p. 145). To improve this situation would take integrity and courage on the parts of both strategy consultants and the executives who hire them.

Raising the bar of business schools was another of Warren's solutions. Shifting the typical business school curriculum toward actual application, particularly in the strategy area, was the strongest recommendation, though admittedly difficult to achieve. The pressure to change the way business schools teach strategy could also come from the students who potentially enroll in their curricula. The demand for applicable skill (are you going to teach me how to actually develop and implement strategy?) as an outcome of these sometimes expensive programs is a reasonable place to start.

Problems with the Practice of Scenario Planning

Scenarios have become a powerful way of thinking about uncertain futures. Scenarios break the assumption that the future can be predicted; that is exactly why they emerged in the first place. And they were developed to compensate for many of the problems with strategic planning (Chermack, 2017; Wack, 1985a). Scenario planning has a much shorter history, with far less application overall, than strategic planning. As a result, the problems are simply smaller and stretch across a much smaller group of professionals than those confronting strategic planning professionals. Scenarios have been successfully used in a variety of industries and sectors. However, scenario planners, too, are guilty of incomplete and ambiguous practice. There are significant opportunities for improvement. For decades, scenario planners have debated methods for developing foresight: the Intuitive Logics school versus the French school versus Cross Impact Matrix Analysis, among many others. Who cares? It is time to move beyond the debates and focus on what has been neglected for so long.

What do you do with scenarios once you have them?

That is, once again, the purpose of this book.

Problems with the practice of scenario planning are in three domains: (1) little or no guidance on how to use scenarios, (2) scenario planning education, and (3) becoming stuck in the practice domain.

Little or No Guidance on Use

The single greatest problem in the practice of scenario planning is the lack of guidance on how to use scenarios.

This problem doesn't require description in detail because it has been fully outlined earlier in the book. The remedy is in the coming chapters and pages. The point is that having scenarios doesn't mean anything if you don't know how to use them.

Scenario Planning Education

Scenarios have historically been taught through a mentor/apprentice relationship. You had to spend time on Shell's famous scenario team or learn scenario planning in one of a few boutique consulting shops that offered training. Currently, there is no existing academic department of scenario planning and no professional organization. There is not a single MBA program that features a concentration in scenario planning. Sure, it may be covered in one session of a strategy course, but that is hardly enough to make someone a competent practitioner. So how do you learn scenario planning? Because it was born in practice (in only a handful of places), scenario planning has no home.

A group of former Shell executives formed the Global Business Network (GBN) and ran it for several years. Their mission was to consult widely on scenario planning and eventually they offered training programs. To this day, a search on LinkedIn will turn up many scenario planning experts who hail from the GBN training. GBN was dissolved in the 2000s; today, to learn scenario planning, you still need a mentor.

There are several books that describe various processes for developing scenarios, and many are excellent. But scenario planning is practiced quite differently depending on where, when, and how the author learned it. The point is not to swing the pendulum toward an MBA degree, where all are taught the same thing and a curriculum is overseen by an accrediting body that tightly controls it. It is important to celebrate the varied approaches to scenarios. And, it might be a benefit to have some convergence toward best practices or agreed-upon competencies.

Futurist Ross Dawson compiled on his website a listing of university futures and foresight degrees and programs, which appears in the appendix of this book. The listing of degrees and programs covers the areas of futures and foresight more generally and is not specific to scenario planning. Some of these programs teach scenario planning, though none features a dedicated focus on it. The one exception is the Oxford Scenarios Programme. While it is not a degree program, it is a full-week training course dedicated to scenarios. The tables in the appendix list the PhD, master's, undergraduate, and short courses related to foresight and futures studies. For brevity, the descriptions listed on Dawson's website have been removed.

Becoming Stuck in the Practice Domain

Scenario planning originated in practice and is an applied realm of activity (Ramirez & Wilkinson, 2016; Schoemaker, 1995; Schwartz, 1996; van der Heijden, 1996). It cannot exist as a pure academic discipline because it requires application to a specific context, industry, and situation. Because it has been so difficult to learn scenario planning, the academic and scientific side has suffered. While there has been increasing research on scenarios, serious attention to outcomes and effectiveness has begun only in the past 10 years. The majority of existing "studies" of scenario planning are most often case descriptions of consulting projects. And most do not identify or describe a legitimate research method (Chermack, 2018). As a result, another challenge put forth in this book is a call for continued research on scenario planning—continued in frequency and rigor and seeking to document the intended outcomes and what it takes to achieve them. Practice reports can be valuable if they are described in a way that gives something back to other scholars and practitioners, but they do not count as scholarship. Think of it this way: it is not acceptable to simply describe an instance of scenario planning. The relevant questions should be the following:

1. What did we do?
2. How did we do it?
3. Did we follow a legitimate research method?
4. What did we learn?
5. Why do we think it was learned?
6. What does it contribute for those wanting evidence that scenario planning is worth the time and effort?

Because scenario planning has not developed rapidly as a discipline in its own right (lacking on the research side for many years), the problems with the practice of scenario planning can be overcome. In fact, they can be overcome much more quickly than the problems with strategic planning. This is because scenario planning does not have a long-embedded history of standardization and academic training. The trend of increased rigor in scenario planning research over the past 10 years is helping, and a challenge put forth in this book is to keep it going.

There is a need to establish continued evidence and scientific rigor that identify and describe precisely what the outcomes of scenario planning are. To move toward more clarity on how to achieve them will only enhance the practice. In short, applied disciplines have to balance practice and research. So far in its history, the practice of scenario planning has far outweighed its research, but the scales are evening out. Continuing to build the academic side of scenario planning, by supporting, promoting, and celebrating *research*, will be important for the discipline to gain credibility.

Future Directions—Readiness

Scenarios have not been widely adopted as a standard business activity. A common question among scenario planners is focused on why the majority of scenario exercises tend to be one-off activities. While some companies do have a long history of scenario use, there certainly aren't many—and none that boasts about its scenario practices the way Shell does. There are several potential explanations for mostly one-off use, and a strong possibility is again that a lack of guidance on how to use scenarios has made many scenario efforts fall short of expectations. Continuing to build the various ways scenarios can be used is critical. Another possible explanation for a lack of widespread uptake in ongoing scenario use is related to readiness.

Scenario planning is more complex than traditional strategic planning, and participants are usually encouraged to think in new and different ways. This can be challenging when compared with the use of standard strategic planning processes (e.g., SWOT analysis) that most people are used to and understand. It is a ripe area to consider that preparation may be required to make scenarios truly successful and adopted for the long term. Experience and anecdotal evidence suggest that readiness in two categories may be important to consider: (1) the organizational resources required (e.g., time, financial support, travel costs, scheduling complexity) and (2) participant psychological readiness (e.g., openness to debate, willingness to consider alternative views, ability to respectfully disagree and still move forward, willingness to question their own mental models). An assessment of organizational and individual readiness could potentially ensure that scenario projects have a much higher likelihood of succeeding and meeting sponsor expectations.

Solutions and Summary

The potential solutions to scenario planning practice problems are relatively clear. This book is entirely aimed at solving the lack of guidance on how to use scenarios. But it won't be the whole solution; in fact, it will probably be a far cry from it. This book is intended to provoke a response in terms of how others are using scenarios. Yes, it is intended to spark a dialogue, and with a little luck, other scenario planning professionals will be willing to show different ways of using scenarios that I have not thought of or covered. The more work we can collectively do in this realm, the more practical and useful scenarios will be.

Scenario planning needs a home. It needs a professional organization—a place for practitioners and scholars to work together. It would be challenging and fun to debate and establish best practices, standards of application, performance outcomes, and maybe even scenario planning competencies. So much important work could be done! Admittedly, the effort required is extensive and the practical minutiae of setting up a professional organization are not that interesting to most scenario planning professionals. However, once established, it could provide the necessary forum for diverse voices in scenario planning to debate these important ideas. Debate and dialogue are the only ways the discipline can evolve and move forward. We ought to apply the advice we give our clients to our own realm of activity.

This chapter has taken a hard look at the reality of how strategic and scenario planning are currently practiced and has put a spotlight on the major difficulties with both. Given the extensive literature available (particularly related to the problems with strategic planning), think of this as a 40,000-foot flyover. This chapter has described the most difficult problems in both domains and, where appropriate, made suggestions for solutions. There are also appropriate citations provided for those who may want to more deeply understand the most recent research on these practice problems.

3 ■ Methods for Building Scenarios

An important challenge and opportunity in scenario planning is that there are different ways to build scenarios. Methods have evolved and developed over the years, and each involves different choices, philosophies, and intended outcomes. For example, it is easy to spend a few hours roughing out some scenario sketches, and these scenarios can be useful for certain purposes. It is also possible to spend eight months or more working out highly detailed and technically brilliant scenarios, complete with systems dynamics, economic modeling, and other analytic support pieces. To be clear, there is significant variation in method. It is the opposite problem of the highly rigid MBA curriculum—every scenario planner likely uses at least a slightly different approach. There is no accrediting agency to oversee standards of scenario planning education, and there is little discussion of competencies or standards of practice. Even the academic scenario planning literature features debates about methodological chaos (Chermack, 2019; Spaniol & Rowland, 2018; Varum & Melo, 2010).

The purpose of this chapter is to present some of the most common scenario planning methods and to show that there is no right way. This chapter contains brief descriptions of several well-known and often used scenario building methods. There is not enough detail for this chapter to be a how-to guide, and it is not intended to be entirely comprehensive. This chapter does not delve into other foresight methods (e.g., backcasting, design futures, or forecasting); the point is to focus on the methods that are available for building scenarios and to provide brief descriptions of them.

Methods for building scenarios generally fall into three categories:

1. Methods that do not focus on the 2×2 matrix method or promote any kind of stepped structure
2. Methods that rely on the 2×2 matrix method or some variation of it
3. Methods that are difficult to classify and report a relatively unique or specialized approach

All of the methods described in this chapter are appropriate for building scenarios.

As you read through this chapter, keep these points in mind:

- The purpose of this book is to recognize that having scenarios doesn't mean anything if you don't know how to use them.
- It doesn't matter how you develop your scenarios, though purpose, expertise, and rigor of thinking count!

Before getting into the various scenario planning methods, it is useful to consider one of the last contributions of Pierre Wack. In brief, Wack was an originator of scenario planning at Shell from 1965 to 1982. His work (along with the support of extensive teams over the years) has established a foundation for scenarios (Chermack, 2017). At the end of a 20-year career at Shell, Wack was given from 1980 to 1982 to document what he had learned as the head of the scenario team for over a decade. His last years at Shell involved traveling to the operating companies around the world to deliver his

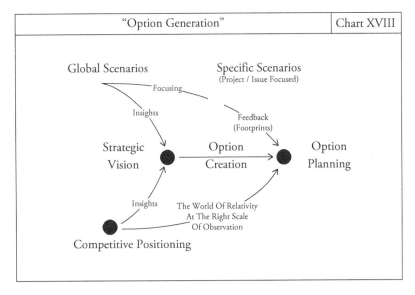

Figure 3.1. Pierre Wack's "Option Generation" (1985b, p. 89)

final scenario reports. On completion of his presentations, he retired from Shell and took a two-year visiting professor position at Harvard Business School. He was there from 1982 to 1984, and during that time he wrote two articles for the *Harvard Business Review*, both of which won McKinsey awards in 1985.

Toward the end of his second *HBR* article, Wack presented a cryptic diagram accompanied by two paragraphs of explanation, which were entirely unsatisfactory. The diagram is in figure 3.1.

Several scholars and practitioners of scenario planning have attempted to interpret Wack's conceptual model of scenario planning given the lack of clarity he offered. As you consider the approaches to building scenarios presented in this chapter, be aware that some clearly involve elements from Wack's original work. This is not intended as a criticism; rather, these approaches are included in order to highlight the fact that Wack's contributions continue to influence even the most modern scenario building approaches. The careful observer will detect many elements of his diagram in the methods described below.

Overview

The first section of this chapter covers the approaches to building scenarios that do not rely on the 2×2 matrix method (though they all make room for it). These methods do not advocate for any stepped approach to scenarios, and they avoid any claims of a "right way" to build scenarios. They include the following:

- The Oxford Scenario Planning Approach
- Van der Heijden's Scenarios: The Art of Strategic Conversation
- Kahane's Transformative Scenario Planning

Each of these is reviewed in terms of its foundational concepts and underlying premises. The goal is not to show you how to apply each of these approaches but to demonstrate some of the different ways you can build scenarios, given the perspectives the authors have taken.

The second section of this chapter describes the basics of several scenario building methods based on the 2×2 matrix method. These include the following:

- The Original 2×2 Matrix Method by Schwartz and Ogilvy
- Wade's Field Guide to the Future Method
- Schoemaker's 10-Step Method
- De Ruijter's 8-Step Method
- Lindgren and Bandhold's TAIDA Method
- Ralston and Wilson's 18-Step Method

The third section of this chapter describes unique scenario building methods that lie outside the classification of the 2×2 matrix method. The methods reviewed in this section are the following:

- Porter's Industry Scenarios
- Godet's "French School"
- Dator's Four Futures

The chapter concludes by summarizing the main points that can be learned from reviewing these methods and what they mean for how to use and apply scenarios.

The Oxford Scenario Planning Approach (OSPA)

The Oxford Scenarios Programme began in 2003 under the direction of Rafael Ramirez and Angela Wilkinson. It is a weeklong scenario training program and offers probably the most customized approach to scenario planning. Drawing from almost 20 years of observation, reflection, and insight, the OSPA is based on a high degree of professional practice, expertise, and research.

In *Strategic Reframing: The Oxford Scenario Planning Approach*, Ramirez and Wilkinson (2016) documented their approach to scenario planning they teach in the program. Ramirez and Wilkinson make it clear they do not advocate for any particular set of steps, processes, or methods. "We are convinced there is *no single best or right method* or set of techniques or tools comprising 'the' method in scenario planning. The OSPA is really more of a methodology than a method. Instead, it is advisable to understand and navigate the methodological choices in designing an intervention that effectively supports the purpose and capabilities of the specific scenario learner" (Ramirez & Wilkinson, 2016, p. 19). The OSPA rests on *designing* a customized scenario experience tailored to the learners and the purposes of the project. Ramirez and Wilkinson describe three foundational concepts that support the OSPA: reframing, turbulence, and TUNA.

Reframing

Drawing from Rein and Shon (1991), Ramirez and Wilkinson position belief systems, perception, and the underlying structure (what they call "frames") as central to scenario planning. These frames influence how people make sense of the world and, therefore, how they engage in it. The OSPA is an iterative approach that positions scenario planning as a way to "reframe strategy and reperceive options for action" (Ramirez & Wilkinson, 2016, p. 5). At the core of the OSPA is the idea that the scenario process can allow participants to experience insights that help them see the context and situation in a different way. Reframing can generally be defined as the ability to identify your own assumptions and understand where and how they could be wrong.

Turbulence—Causal Texture Theory

Emery and Trist's (1965) classic work was the first to describe "turbulent field environments" or contexts involving high degrees of change with the potential to fundamentally alter the environment or situation. They explained the "causal texture" (p. 18) of the environment, suggesting that the combination of a high rate of change and complexity leads to high uncertainty. The OSPA puts these concepts at the heart of scenarios and how they can be used to navigate such turbulent environments. Scenarios are meant to help participants and decision makers understand the factors and forces that are underneath the change and complexity that create unstable and uncertain environments.

TUNA (Turbulence, Uncertainty, Novelty, and Ambiguity)

In addition to turbulence, uncertainty, novelty, and ambiguity are conditions of the environment that make it difficult to understand and navigate. Uncertainty is a given by-product of turbulence in the environment as established by Emery and Trist (1965). Turbulence and uncertainty are standard features of the environments that scenarios are usually built to understand more deeply. Novelty and ambiguity require more explanation.

Novelty

The Oxford English Dictionary defines novelty as "the quality of being new, original, or unusual" (1989, p. 367). Ramirez and Wilkinson (2016) offer examples of what they describe as novel developments in various situations:

> The convergence of new computer enhanced technologies— including nanotechnology, artificial intelligence, biochemistry, robotics, programming and communication—heralds for some a new era of self-generated work "local capitalism" and "circular economy" that may become very different in scale, speed, and nature from both the recent era of global financial capitalism and earlier industrial-scale job creation. (p. 30)

Another, more specific example clarifies the point: "Indeed, Henry Ford purportedly commented that if he had asked people what they wanted they would have said 'faster horses,' but what he imagined and realized with the mass production of the automobile resulted in a new culture of consumerism" (Ramirez & Wilkinson, 2016, p. 31). This example makes it clear how novelty can apply when thinking strategically. To think beyond what others can conceive—and to be able to deliver on it—clearly captures the spirit of novelty.

Ambiguity

"Ambiguity arises when there are different interpretations of the same event or phenomenon. In the OSPA, the aim is not immediately to resolve ambiguity to facilitate problem solving" (Ramirez & Wilkinson, 2016, p. 31). According to the Oxford English Dictionary, ambiguity is defined as "the quality of being open to interpretation, inexactness" (1989, p. 119). Of course, there is no precise answer for how to think about the future or strategy work. Human perception is at the center of how organizations create, develop, and design their strategies (Mintzberg et al., 2020), and ambiguity is consistently a part of that process.

With these foundational concepts in place, the OSPA has seven key premises, as identified by the authors:

1. Many organizations are facing unprecedented TUNA conditions.
2. TUNA conditions require new approaches to strategic and policy planning that seek to balance competitive and collaborative opportunities.
3. Intent to develop an explicit and flexible sense of future contexts through an iterative process of reframing and reperception.
4. The "aha" moment of impact is only realized once the reframing-reperception cycle has been completed. This can require several iterations.
5. A culture of learning supported by scenario planning can avoid the extremes of groupthink and fragmentation, which are pathologies preventing learning in organizational settings.

6. Reframing strategy is a distinctive capability that enables learners to identify new opportunities and more and better options.
7. Scenario planning can help develop new social capital to renew the license to operate.

These seven premises are the foundational assumptions of the OSPA. The degree to which a practitioner understands these assumptions in the target environment is vital to the scenario experience for participants. The authors stress a focus on designing an intervention tailored to the learning experiences of the participants.

OSPA Method Choices

The OSPA does not recommend any specific procedural component; rather, it focuses on the variety of choices available to the scenario planner and makes room for the pros and cons of each. While the scenario planner is free to choose among many different intervention options, the OSPA is a set of approaches to scenario planning that can be decided based on purpose, use, and users. These intervention choices include the following:

- Deductive method
- Inductive method
- Abductive method
- Normative method
- Incremental method
- Alternative futures method
- Critical scenarios method
- Perspectives-based method

Because of its extensive flexibility, the OSPA requires some elaboration on each of these choices. The deductive method generally refers to studying the external environment and distilling that study down to the most critical uncertainties in the local environment. This is, essentially, the 2×2 matrix method. It is macro to micro. The inductive method starts with identifying unique factors in the immediate environment and extending them into larger questions about trends and uncertain factors at a larger scale. It is micro to macro. The abductive approach combines the two. Essentially, it allows for the explanation of the micro environment as a consequence of what happens in the macro environment. Essentially, they work together and have to be logically connected. Although generally uncommon in scenario planning, the normative method is important because it introduces the idea of intention. These scenarios are based on how we want the future to be. Ogilvy's (2002) work is precisely in this category, and while normative scenario planning is usually applied to longer-term efforts (e.g., climate change or global sustainability), there are certainly instances of desired futures applied in the shorter term (see Kahane, 2004, 2012).

The incremental method comes from Pierre Wack at Shell in the 1960s (Wack, 1985b). He realized that presenting executives with scenarios that contained dramatically challenging futures needed some softening. His approach was to extend the current reality as a "status quo" scenario into the future and then show how it simply couldn't last. Once he was able to show that the current reality was not sustainable, he would then present the more challenging alternative scenarios. This approach can be used with the 2×2 or any other scenario method. It can be a useful tool in showing that the status quo cannot survive. The alternative futures method was developed by Jim Dator in 1981. The framework includes four standard scenarios (of course adjusted to the context) and the general themes are "Growth," "Collapse," "Conservation," and "Transformation." These themes could be applied to almost any situation, relieving the scenario planner of customized work related to the particular organizational/environmental context. The critical scenarios method focuses on power relations (Inayatullah, 1998, 2002). The target of this approach to scenarios is to uncover limiting power structures in organizations and societies with a firm effort toward changing them. Finally, Ramirez and Wilkinson describe the perspectives-based approach. In this method, the point of scenario planning is to "reveal and navigate between differing world-views, and within world-views to reveal their assumptions and help those who hold them to accommodate different perspectives" (Ramirez & Wilkinson, 2016, p. 118).

The OSPA is highly flexible and requires extensive experience to apply. This is because of the choices presented to the scenario planner. The OSPA includes minimal formal guidance or structure, which means the scenarios that are built can vary widely according to the choices made. Essentially, the choices made by the scenario planner about which process or method to use are highly tailored to the situation and context of the scenario planning intervention.

Van der Heijden—*Scenarios: The Art of Strategic Conversation*

Scenarios: The Art of Strategic Conversation was published in 1996. The author—Kees van der Heijden—was an understudy of Pierre Wack's at Shell, and he was asked to learn as much as he could before Wack retired in 1982. Van der Heijden went on to lead Shell's scenario team from 1989 to 1991. His exposure and expertise related to scenario planning are second to none. The approach focuses on the development of a context for scenario planning and a philosophical tour around why leaders may want to use scenario planning in the first place. A single chapter is dedicated to scenario development, and the descriptions (like the OSPA) allow the scenario planning facilitator a high degree of freedom. Attention is given to the scenario team, novelty, data analysis, and historical study. The importance of identifying "driving forces" is clear, and as with the OSPA, the primary differentiation is between inductive, deductive, and incremental scenario development.

Inductive Scenario Building

According to van der Heijden, the inductive approach begins with the identification of events. "In the inductive method the approach builds step by step on the data available and allows the structure of the scenarios to emerge by itself" (van der Heijden, 1996, p. 196). Events and what-ifs drive the development of a few storylines that emerge from data on up. In the inductive approach, a scenario planner begins by identifying the major forces, "fitting" the data into where they make the most sense. Often in cases of inductive scenario building, a major uncertainty is selected as the primary theme of the scenario, and supporting details for how that uncertainty could evolve are sought through additional research (Konno et al., 2014). When working with a set of scenarios and using the inductive method, it is common for each scenario to be built on a different major theme. The task then becomes making sure that the scenarios do not overlap too much, but also stick together as a set.

Deductive Scenario Building

In the discussion of the deductive method, van der Heijden includes attention to the 2 × 2 and 2 × 2×2 approaches (the 2 × 2×2 approach involves a third axis). In these cases, under the deductive method, scenarios are developed along the track of two or three structural variables that frame the scenarios. Data, interviews, and additional research are used to fill in the stories within the frames. These scenarios begin with a framework deduced from participant input and proceed to supplement the scenario work with additional research, study, and insights gained from the interviews. Like the OSPA, van der Heijden's approach also allows for the use of the 2 × 2 matrix method.

Incremental Scenario Building

Van der Heijden did give some attention to the incremental method. "This approach aims lower and is useful if the client team still needs to be convinced that the scenario approach offers an opportunity to enhance the strategic conversation" (van der Heijden, 1996, p. 196). Here again, the idea of an official future is emphasized. The official future is the status quo: the business-as-usual scenario taken forward. It is easy to show many ways that the current reality cannot hold, and it is sometimes a clever idea to provide a single status quo scenario and tear it apart. This approach can make it clear to skeptics that the current reality simply cannot last, and opens the door to look at truly alternative scenarios.

The Business Idea

Van der Heijden's most important contribution is his description of the business idea. This is a simple systems diagram intended to portray the actual system by which the organization lives its life (van der Heijden, 2005). It is one of very few applications of systems thinking as a pre-activity to scenario planning. The core of the idea is that it is first important to understand a need in society and then to carry it through to a needed product or service. What makes firms different from one another is the realization of a distinctive resource or competency that cannot be easily replicated. There are so many examples of firms that have carved out a space in which they deliver a value along with something new (e.g., Southwest Airlines or Amazon). Yet van der Heijden's premise is that most companies do not have a clear picture of (1) a need identified in society, (2) a unique product or service that is beyond what is currently offered, and (3) the ability to use resources to deliver something new.

Many leaders assume they are aligned on the general business idea, and this assumption is not often checked. Asking the executive team to draw their individual business models results in wildly different interpretations, and it can be a useful activity. Comparing them is an exercise in dealing with mental models. The result is usually an extremely productive conversation about exactly why the organization is in business, what needs it serves, generally how it meets those needs, and the critical mechanisms required to deliver its products or services.

Kahane: Evolving the Scenario Method

Adam Kahane was a principal on the scenario team at Shell from 1981 to 1993 (Wilkinson & Kupers, 2014). He worked under scenario team leaders and Kees van der Heijden (1989–1991) and Joseph Jaworski (1991–1993). In his first book, *Solving Tough Problems* (2004), Kahane describes several instances of scenario planning in large-scale sociopolitical contexts, including the famous Mont Fleur scenarios focused on the future of South Africa (1992). As the title implies, what is unique about Kahane's contribution is the setting: he applies scenario planning (with adjustment and customization) to wide-ranging problems, often at the community, state, or even national level, with an intent to change and transform systems. Because of the emphasis on changing systems that are understood to be problematic, the approach could be classified as normative scenario planning—bringing in the idea of intention and how the group wants the future to be. Transformative scenarios are constructed to create a better future, a desired future. In addition, transformative scenarios are also constructed through never talking about a desired future (except at the very end of the process).

The book is written in story format, and the descriptions of the scenario planning process are vague. Kahane describes a series of workshops involving brainstorming in small, diverse groups that represented many, if not all, major stakeholders in the future of South Africa. The focus was "to talk not about what they or their party wanted to happen—their usual way of talking about the future—but simply about what might happen, regardless of what they wanted" (Kahane, 2004, p. 21). The brainstorming workshops continued over several days. "The first brainstorming exercise produced thirty stories. The team combined these and narrowed them down to nine for further work" (Kahane, 2004, p. 22). Kahane describes an iterative process of brainstorming to create storylines and then refining them into a final set of four over the course of almost a year. He has documented the application of scenario planning to problematic situations and systems throughout the Americas, Europe, the Middle East, and Asia.

Transformative Scenario Planning

In his book *Transformative Scenario Planning*, Kahane (2012) sets out a slightly more structured process that includes the following phases:

1. Convene a team from across the whole system
2. Observe what is happening
3. Construct stories about what could happen
4. Discover what can and must be done
5. Act to transform the system

Within these phases, Kahane stresses the importance of team member selection. Diversity of background, ways of thinking, ethnicity, position, and role are critically important. The idea is to gain representation from all parts of the system. In phase two, several suggestions are made for observing, including the selection of meeting locations, traveling as a team to observe different parts of the system, inviting representatives from different parts of the system to make presentations, and self-observation of the team, among several others. The intended outcome is to use as many different perspectives as possible to gain a shared understanding of the system. In phase three, as with the OSPA and van der Heijden's framework, Kahane leaves room for the possible use of the 2×2 matrix method through the deductive method. However, most of his examples come from the application of the inductive method. "Neither of these methods is mechanical; both require you to make a judgment about which of the many possible stories are the most useful ones" (Kahane, 2012, p. 58). The descriptions provided for how to build scenarios are not lengthy or detailed, leaving a lot of the complications that can arise from either method not fully developed. According to Kahane, sometimes a 2×2 matrix can be an ex post way to represent a set of scenarios that were developed using another method, which allows even more flexibility in terms of the choice of method.

The fourth phase involves the team coming to a shared understanding of what can and must be done to change the system. Kahane promoted journaling, quiet time, reflection, meditation, and other personal activities to interrupt the process and force it to shut down (temporarily) as highly productive and creative. Once the team has had some time for reflection, an adaptive stance is applied. "The adaptive stance assumes you cannot change the system you are part of and implies that you must accept it and adapt to it" (Kahane, 2012, p. 66). This is followed by applying the transformative stance, which "assumes that you can change the system (in most cases through allying with others) and implies that you must try to do so courageously" (p. 66). Applying these stances with additional reflection allows the team to arrive at the final step, which is acting to transform the system. "These actions can take any number of forms: campaigns, meetings, movements, publications, projects, policies, initiatives, institutions, or legislation; private or public; short-term or long-term"

(p. 69). Kahane's major contribution is demonstrating the use of scenarios in large-scale, sociopolitical issues with an aim to understand a system and how to change it.

Summary

These three scenario planning methods promote extensive freedom in designing and delivering scenario planning interventions. The texts do not provide a lot of detailed guidance for the novice—these are not methods an emerging scenario planner could read and apply. They assume levels of experience and competence from the start. Facilitators have numerous choices in how the scenario experience is designed and delivered for clients, and these three methods all highlight choice over detailed process. These approaches require expertise in learning design, facilitation, and negotiation and in understanding client needs and organization development overall. These require the scenario planner to be confident and expert in the choices made throughout. They are truly customized approaches, and as we have seen, they can include the 2 × 2 matrix method. The needs of the scenario learners and clients, expected outcomes, and how the scenarios are intended to be used are critically important and usually drive decisions about the details for how to approach scenario building.

The 2 × 2 Matrix Method

There is a lot of confusion about the origin of the 2 × 2 matrix method. All evidence points to a short appendix in the second edition of Peter Schwartz's *The Art of the Long View*, published in 1996. In 1996, Schwartz was the president of the Global Business Network. GBN was founded in 1987 by Peter Schwartz, Jay Ogilvy, Stewart Brand, Lawrence Wilkinson, and Napier Collyns (Schwartz, 2012). Both Schwartz and Collyns had previous careers with Shell, and in fact, Schwartz was the successor to the legendary Pierre Wack as the head of the scenarios team (1982–1986). By 1996, GBN was a highly successful consulting company delivering scenario planning to some of the world's largest corporations. They also started offering week-long scenario training programs with the goal of teaching people how to do it. The evidence suggests that it was a collaboration between Schwartz and Ogilvy that led to the 2 × 2 matrix method, as they published an article on the GBN website that also appeared in 1996. This became the basis for their training program. The appendix of *The Art of the Long View* lists the steps of the 2 × 2 matrix method as follows (Schwartz 1996, p. 241):

1. Identify focal issue or decision
2. Key forces in the local environment
3. Driving forces
4. Rank by importance and uncertainty
5. Selecting scenario logics
6. Fleshing out the scenarios
7. Implications
8. Selection of leading indicators and signposts

Most readers will be familiar with this general scenario building method. There is no need to describe these steps in detail; however, many scenario consultants and authors have slightly reinterpreted the original method. Each of these is reviewed in brief, and this chapter makes it clear that many scenario building methods are simple variations on Schwartz and Ogilvy's original contribution. Relevant interpretations of the 2 × 2 matrix method are each authored by specific people: Woody Wade, Paul Schoemaker, Paul de Ruijter, Mats Lindgren and Hans Bandhold, and Bill Ralston and Ian Wilson.

Woody Wade: *A Field Guide to the Future*

Wade has over 30 years of business experience, having spent significant time in the banking industry and with the World Economic Forum. In his book *Scenario Planning: A Field Guide to the Future*, Wade wrote, "There is no fixed, Here's-how-you-do-it rulebook for conducting a scenario planning process or workshop" (2012, p. 29).

Wade went on to describe the following six steps, which clearly reflect a basis in the 2 × 2 matrix method:

1. Framing the challenge
2. Gathering information
3. Identifying driving forces
4. Defining the future's critical "either/or" uncertainties
5. Generating the scenarios
6. Fleshing them out and creating storylines

These steps are essentially the same as those defined by Schwartz and Ogilvy in 1996. Wade's contribution is more of a picture book, with many pages featuring a simple quote and many full-page pictures. The discussion of "defining the critical, either/or uncertainties" (Wade, 2012, p. 85) showcases the 2 × 2 matrix, and every example included in the book is based on it. The book is generally light on content and doesn't provide detailed descriptions of the various steps—certainly not enough to apply it.

Paul Schoemaker: Decision Strategies International

Schoemaker's background includes some time at Shell, among many other companies. He also served for a decade as the research director of the Mack Center for Technological Innovation at the Wharton School, University of Pennsylvania. He founded Decision Strategies International (DSI) in 1990, which was sold to Heidrick & Struggles in 2016. Schoemaker describes 10 steps to scenario planning in his seminal 1995 article "Scenario Planning: A Tool for Strategic Thinking," which also formed the basis of DSI's consulting approach for over 25 years. The steps are as follows:

1. Define the scope
2. Identify major stakeholders
3. Identify basic trends
4. Identify key uncertainties
5. Construct initial scenario themes

6. Check for consistency and plausibility
7. Develop learning scenarios
8. Identify research needs
9. Develop quantitative models
10. Evolve toward decision scenarios

Again, there is little to differentiate his 10 steps from any other approach under the 2 × 2 matrix method, except for breaking them down into further detail. For example, step 2 deals exclusively with identifying stakeholders and participants. This is an important highlight, and Schoemaker's experience has informed his separation of the steps into more discrete activities as a result (Schoemaker, 2012, 2019). Step 5 deals with initial scenario construction, and Schoemaker wrote, "Select the top two uncertainties and cross them" (1995, p. 29), which is the defining feature to identify it as being based on the 2 × 2 method. While Schoemaker's description includes attention to "developing quantitative models" and "evolving toward decision scenarios," there are no examples, instructions, or detailed guides for how to practice and apply these tools.

Paul de Ruijter: *Scenario-Based Strategy*

After spending time with Group Planning at Shell in London, de Ruijter used the scenario method with the Royal Netherlands Academy of Arts and Sciences. Eventually, he went on to start his own shop (De Ruijter Strategy) and divides his time between consulting and lecturing at Nyenrode University, Delft University, and the University of Amsterdam. Based on his experience, de Ruijter's 2014 book *Scenario-Based Strategy: Navigate the Future* presents eight steps to the scenario planning process:

1. Mission
2. Trends
3. Scenarios
4. Options
5. Vision
6. Road map

7. Action
8. Monitoring

While a descriptive guide, de Ruijter's book avoids discrete steps. Though it leans firmly in the direction of the methods that rely on the 2 × 2 matrix method, there is some description of the inductive scenario approach. As with other method descriptions, minimal guidance is offered for applying the inductive method. In step three—scenarios—de Ruijter describes a possibility for non–2 × 2 matrix approaches, though the examples offered in his book generally follow the 2 × 2 matrix method. While the cases are brief, they provide examples of applied, real scenario planning. De Ruijter's method pays attention to the importance of options and identifying possible actions. These possible actions are then windtunneled through the scenarios. "In practice, you can do this by taking existing plans as a starting point and then checking for each scenario whether or not (1) goals are feasible, (2) budgets are either too high or too low, and (3) activities should be brought forward, postponed, started or stopped given the specific conditions of the scenarios" (de Ruijter, 2014, p. 88). There is also some attention to what he calls "Robust, Call and Put Options" (p. 91), though the examples are not detailed enough to translate into practice. De Ruijter's method provides examples and guidance throughout the scenario building process. Further detail on precisely how to apply the concepts after the scenarios are built would boost the utility of his method.

Mats Lindgren and Hans Bandhold: *Scenario Planning: The Link between Future and Strategy*

Lindgren and Bandhold are senior partners at Kairos Future, a leading consultancy in Scandinavia. The authors published *Scenario Planning: The Link between Future and Strategy* in 2003, which is based on almost four decades of combined experience. In it, they develop what they call the TAIDA method of scenario planning:

1. Tracking
2. Analyzing

3. Imaging
4. Deciding
5. Acting

These various phases follow the same activities as the other approaches based on the 2 × 2 method. Tracking involves finding trends and uncertainties, gathering information, and understanding the industry. Trends and drivers are considered in terms of their impact on the issue and their predictability to prioritize trends. The analyzing phase requires developing an understanding of how the various drivers and trends may interact with and influence each other. It also features selecting different combinations of uncertainties to create what they call a scenario "cross" (matrix) (Lindgren & Bandhold, 2003, p. 67). The analyzing phase includes developing written scenarios based on logically connecting various other dynamics that emerged in the tracking phase. The next phase—imaging—describes the development of an internal vision. This is the future that leaders aspire to achieve and puts preferences into the planning activity. With a vision in place, the deciding phase is next. Having tracked what is happening in the external environment, analyzing it in the form of four scenarios, and then developing a vision, the deciding phase focuses on what actions are available to move in the direction of the vision, keeping in mind the context of the tracking and analyzing phases.

The TAIDA method makes some suggestions about going beyond the work required to make scenarios, though practical details are missing. The deciding and acting phases are far too vague to be applied, and any user is left to interpret and create something useful. The tracking, analyzing, and imaging phases, which map almost exactly to the other methods based on Schwartz's original description in *The Art of the Long View*, provide advice for building scenarios.

Bill Ralston and Ian Wilson: *The Scenario Planning Handbook*

Ralston and Wilson are seasoned strategy and scenario professionals. Coming out of a long career with the Stanford Research Institute

(SRI), Ralston held positions with SRI Business Intelligence and SRI International and went on to found PGO Consulting. Wilson spent 25 years at General Electric in strategy and human resources (where he and Pierre Wack had exchanges in the 1980s) and then worked as a consultant at SRI. In 2006, having met and worked together at SRI for several years, they coauthored *The Scenario Planning Handbook*. In it, they provide 18 steps for scenario planning:

1. Developing the case for scenarios
2. Gaining executive understanding, support, and participation
3. Defining the decision focus
4. Designing the process
5. Selecting the facilitator
6. Forming the scenario team
7. Gathering available data, views, and projections
8. Identifying and assessing key decision factors
9. Identifying the critical forces and drivers
10. Conducting focused research
11. Assessing the importance and predictability/uncertainty of forces and drivers
12. Identifying the key axes of uncertainty
13. Selecting scenario logics to cover the envelope of uncertainty
14. Writing the storylines for the scenarios
15. Rehearsing the future with scenarios
16. Getting to the decision recommendations
17. Identifying the signposts to monitor
18. Communicating the results to the organization

Wilson and Ralston provide the most detailed description of scenario building. Their steps break the process down even further. Even though there is more detail in how they have divided the steps, the general 2×2 matrix method from Schwartz is clearly the foundation. Ralston and Wilson start at the beginning, creating a case for scenario planning and for how to convince decision makers that it is a useful activity. Attention is given to the facilitator, the team, gathering different views across the organization, and understanding important dynamics in the environment. All of this leads to steps 11 and 12—some kind of ranking process for importance and predictability and then identifying the two key axes of uncertainty.

The method extends beyond building scenarios and provides some hints for how to use them. There are two chapters focused on using the scenarios to think about the future and work toward decision recommendations. However, what is offered in a small number of pages is not adequate for those looking to apply the activities described.

Summary of the 2 × 2 Scenario Matrix Method

By now, you should be able to recognize the common parts of scenario building approaches that rely on the 2 × 2 matrix method. After reviewing these versions of the 2 × 2 matrix method, it should be clear that there isn't that much difference among them. There are slight nuances—for example, different criteria for ranking key uncertainties could be "importance and uncertainty," "impact and uncertainty," or "importance and predictability" depending on a given author's specific preference. On the one hand, you could argue that these are just semantics. On the other, you could argue that these words and concepts matter; importance is really different from impact, and uncertainty is really different from predictability. The point is not to resolve these issues in this chapter but only to highlight the variation in methods for building scenarios, right down to the words that vary among practitioners. The point is that any way you cut it, if the method ultimately arrives at determining two critical uncertainties put on a matrix, you are working with the 2 × 2 method.

Notes on the 2 × 2 Matrix Method

Many wrongly attribute the 2 × 2 matrix method to Shell, perhaps because so many Shell alumni use it. It is true that Pierre Wack (one of Shell's most famous scenario planning gurus) used two 2 × 2 matrices—but only two—in his almost 30-year career. The first matrix Wack used was to frame some early scenarios while he worked for Shell Francaise, before he went to London to officially work on

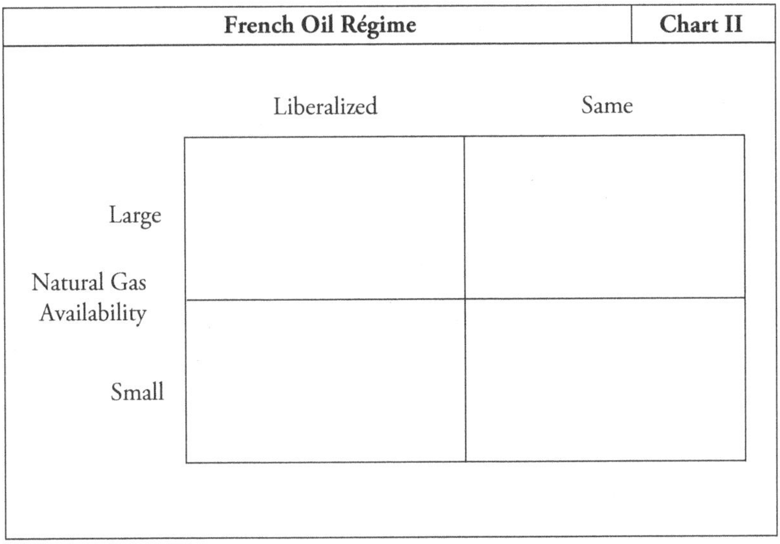

French Oil Régime		Chart II
	Liberalized	Same
Large		
Natural Gas Availability		
Small		

Figure 3.2. Wack's First 2 × 2 Matrix (Wack, 1985a)

the scenario team. It was 1968, and Shell was engaged in a long-term planning project known as the Horizon Year Planning Exercise. At the time, Wack was the director of economics for Shell Francaise, and he was asked to lead the project for the Paris office (Chermack, 2017). The matrix he produced was relatively simple: on the x axis was "natural gas availability," and on the y axis was whether France's oil regime would liberalize or stay the same (see figure 3.2).

This matrix was not the result of any kind of sticky note exercise, and there are no surviving notes to suggest how or why he selected these as important variables. It is not clear why or how he developed this matrix. It seems intuitive that based on his understanding of the context, the two variables he selected were highly uncertain.

The second matrix he used was to classify major oil exporters. Thus, it cannot really be called a scenario matrix in the traditional sense because it was not used to build scenarios. In this case, "absorptive capacity" and "reserves" were selected for the axes (again without explanation), and the matrix was used to classify where the major oil-producing countries would fall within the quadrants (see figure 3.3).

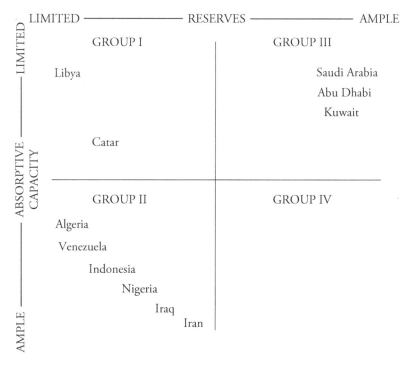

Figure 3.3. Major Oil Exporters (Wack 1985a)

Some Practical Advice on the 2 × 2 Matrix Method

As a primary method, experience has taught a few important lessons in using the 2 × 2 matrix method over many years. Some practical advice for parts of scenario building that require some care includes dealing with leadership involvement, the composition of the participant group, how to label the ends of the axes in a scenario matrix, and a particular thought on using the economy as one of the axes.

First, plain and simple, scenario building gets much more traction when leaders are involved. Leadership presence (or the lack of it) sends a critical message to the rest of the team. Certainly, leaders are busy people, and nothing will change the tone of the scenario building work more than leaders being called away for some kind of emergency, never to return, or delegating the work down the hierarchy.

The composition of the scenario participant group is also critical. Participants need to be willing to engage and speak their minds, be able to respectfully disagree and still move forward, understand that consensus is not necessary, and finally, have a diverse set of perspectives on the focus of the scenario work. Care and thoughtfulness in selecting participants will pay dividends throughout the scenario building activities and beyond. All of this speaks to the potential importance of readiness discussed in the previous chapter.

There has been some discussion in the literature about how to label the ends of the axes in a scenario matrix (Gordon, 2020). One suggestion is to consider whether to use the matrix as a grid or frames (Ramirez & Wilkinson, 2014). Figures 3.4 and 3.5 demonstrate the idea.

These two ways of viewing the scenario matrix provide two different approaches to labeling the ends of the axes. The pros and cons of each are discussed, and the practitioner is left to make a selection based on what best fits the particular situation. One caution is that the "on/off, yes/no" approach can easily involve absolutes that lead to good, bad, and status quo scenarios. Being more creative about how to label the ends of the axes creates more interesting scenarios. The world does not evolve in strictly positive or negative ways.

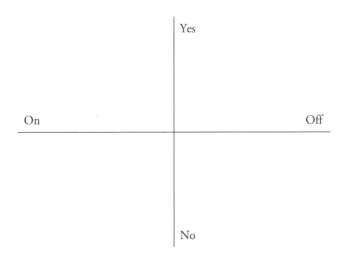

Figure 3.4. The Scenario Matrix as a Grid (Ramirez & Wilkinson, 2014)

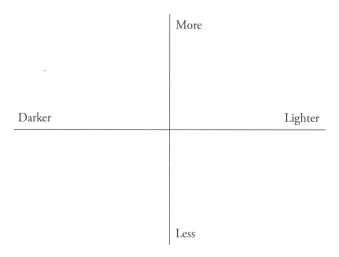

Figure 3.5. The Scenario Matrix as Frames (Ramirez & Wilkinson, 2014)

A further suggestion based on extensive experiences is to make the ends of the axes *qualitatively different*. This approach has produced the best results and the most interesting scenarios. Describing the ends of each axis with three or four bullet descriptors (rather than a single word) changes this part of the process dramatically. It also begins to shape the scenarios in more interesting ways than using a single label because you are trying to describe two different possible extremes rather than something good or something bad.

Unique Scenario Building Methods

Now that the two major schools of scenario building have been reviewed, three other specific methods need mention:

- Porter's Industry Scenarios
- Godet's "French School"
- Dator's "Four Futures"

These scenario building methods have long histories and represent unique and fundamentally different approaches. Again, the purpose is not to describe these methods at the level of detail required for application; it is to provide awareness and highlight three more long-standing options for scenario building.

Porter's Industry Scenarios

Porter's (1980, 1985a) work on competitive strategy included some attention to scenarios. Porter generally did not support scenarios focused on specific business issues, divisions, or business units; instead, he focused specifically on industry scenarios. Industry scenarios are based on macroeconomic and macropolitical issues. "In competitive strategy, the appropriate unit for the analysis of scenarios is the industry—I term such scenarios *industry* scenarios. Industry scenarios allow a firm to translate uncertainty into its strategic implications for a particular industry" (Porter, 1985a, p. 447). By focusing on the industry as the unit of analysis, scenarios can be generated that consider disruptive innovations, potential competitor behaviors, and how markets could shift dramatically.

The process of constructing industry scenarios requires the following steps:

- Identify the uncertainties that may affect industry structure
- Determine the causal factors driving them
- Make a range of plausible assumptions about each important causal factor
- Combine assumptions about individual factors into internally consistent scenarios
- Analyze the industry structure that would prevail under each scenario
- Determine the sources of competitive advantage under each scenario
- Predict competitor behavior under each scenario

Porter's approach does not feature the 2 × 2 matrix method and does not even mention the phrase. The focus is shifted toward competition, which is entirely consistent with his work. It is interesting to consider that when Pierre Wack was a visiting professor at the Harvard Business School from 1982 to 1984, his office was across the hall from Porter's. While there are no surviving records of conversations, clearly the two must have had exchanges; competitive positioning appears in Wack's diagram at the start of this chapter, and Porter's book contains a section on scenarios, even though Porter has his own take on them.

The process described of constructing industry scenarios highlights making uncertainty part of the planning process, and the unique contribution is the level of analysis. It is still worth questioning how industry scenarios could be useful for decision making or any other more detailed application (e.g., you cannot get any kind of financial analysis out of a set of industry scenarios).

Industry scenarios are also sometimes called global scenarios (Davis, 2003). Specifically referring to Shell's practices, "global scenarios are a significant part of Shell's planning system, but the more focused application of scenario methodology is also increasingly important for setting local strategy and assessing projects or decisions" (Davis, 2003, p. 67). As you can imagine, developing scenarios for the entire global energy industry means that they cannot possibly be detailed enough for use at a regional or local level. This is why, at least at Shell, a tiered scenario system is preferred. In Shell's case, multiple sets of "sub-scenarios" that use the dynamics of the global scenarios are then customized for regions or business units.

Godet's "French School"

Michel Godet is a professor and holds the Chair of Strategic Prospective at the National Conservatory for Arts and Industries in Paris. His work has spanned many decades, and he has been a prolific author and consultant. His work is based on the contributions of Gaston Berger. Steeped in the philosophies of Edmund Husserl, the "French school" of scenario planning is very much based in phenomenology (the study of a given phenomenon) (Godet, 2000, 2001). There is little guidance offered in Godet's works, though three phases are generally defined:

Phase 1: Study internal and external variables
Phase 2: Identify key variables
Phase 3: Develop scenarios

Phase 1 involves understanding internal and external variables and developing an understanding of how they are interrelated. The outputs are then generally described as being input into a database. Attention is given to how each variable influences the others. Phase 2 promotes scanning the data, considering the possibilities, and identifying associated variables and strategies. The next phase is generally described as a process of developing hypotheses based on the trends identified throughout the previous phases. Software can be used to analyze data gathered, and probabilities are assigned to estimate the likelihoods of various possible events. Next comes the actual development of scenarios, which are based on the hypotheses generated from software analyses.

While the examples are detailed and the cases provide specifics in the figures presented, there is little to no guidance on precisely how to accomplish the various outputs that are claimed. The phases are vague, and the advice falls short of providing the kind of structure required to perform the tasks.

Dator's "Four Futures"

Jim Dator is professor emeritus and former director of the Hawaii Research Center for Futures Studies, Department of Political Science, University of Hawaii. His work of over 50 years has shaped the field of futures studies. While his contributions have spanned widely across the field of futures studies, his specific contributions to scenarios were mentioned within the discussion of the Oxford Scenario Planning Approach and require further recognition. Dator's approach was developed in 1981 (see Dator & Bezold, 1981). The approach includes four standard scenarios which are adjusted to the particular contexts in which they are used. The general themes are "Growth," "Collapse," "Conservation," and "Transformation." It should be easy to see that these general scenario themes could be useful as overall archetypes when thinking about the future of any group or organization.

Dator's original approach has been adapted more recently (see Fergnani & Song, 2020; Hines & Bishop, 2013), and these variations are widely used throughout the Asia-Pacific region (based on Dator's extensive work throughout the area). The appeal of a standard set of scenario archetypes is based on the idea that there are storylines that tend to occur again and again, even with custom scenario work. For example, even with the 2 × 2 matrix method, there will commonly be a scenario that is more positive, one that is quite difficult, and two genuine alternatives (see figures 3.4 and 3.5 for how to solve this issue).

Other Scenario Building Concepts

The purpose of this chapter is not to cover scenario building practices and principles in depth. Instead, it is to provide a brief overview of some of the most common scenario building methods. There are, however, several important scenario building concepts that are certainly covered elsewhere, though they are important enough to mention here. People often ask which scenario building method is the best. Many authors and practitioners have been clear that there is no one right way. Still, it is important to make a suggestion for how you might choose a scenario building method. The second important principle has to do with naming scenarios. Some examples are provided along with suggestions for selecting scenario names. Finally, there is the issue of probability, plausibility, and provocation. This refers to how scenarios can be assessed or judged in terms of their utility. These issues are covered briefly as they demonstrate the complexity and choices involved with scenario building once again.

Pros and Cons of Each Method

Some scenario planners talk about the pros and cons of each method. This is not a useful activity, because most scenario planning projects lack a clearly articulated purpose and intended outcomes. The best way to select a specific scenario planning method is to clearly define the purpose of the project and the outcomes sought. As we have already seen, scenarios can be developed to explore environments and what-ifs, or they can be developed specifically to test an organizational strategy. I have argued that there has not been sufficient attention to how to use scenarios once they are created, and again, this book focuses entirely on that topic. The hope is that on review of the seven different ways to use scenarios described in later sections, you will have a much better understanding of different scenario purposes, the ways in which they can be used, and outcomes that *could* be sought. An understanding of the depth and breadth of how scenarios can be used should allow you to make a more informed decision about which scenario building method is best suited to the intent of the project.

On Naming Scenarios

One thing that all scenario approaches have in common, regardless of the method used, is the importance of naming the scenarios. A set of scenarios needs a theme, and within that theme, each scenario needs a name related to the theme. Here are some examples:

Theme: Beatles songs (from Ogilvy & Schwartz, 2004)
  Scenario names
      — A Hard Day's Night
      — Help!
      — Magical Mystery Tour
      — Imagine
Theme: travel technology
  Scenario names
      — SpaceX Falcon 9
      — United B90
      — John Deere
      — Durango Silverton Railway
Theme: animals
  Scenario names
      — Armadillo
      — Alligator
      — Quail
      — Red wolf

Some scenario planners call this "mental velcro." The idea is that the name of the scenario reminds users and participants of its core storyline very quickly. If you were to visit previous clients, they would remember the main storyline of a scenario if you simply said the name. Scenario naming is a very powerful device, and strategies for considering names could include geographic features in the local environment (e.g., a statewide scenario project could consider rivers or mountain ranges) or products relevant to the industry (e.g., different kinds of cars), among others. A practical way to facilitate this is to assign participants to groups of four or five people, ask each group to generate a theme and scenario names, and then have everyone vote on a final selection. This is a highly creative, fun, and energizing part of the process.

Probability, Plausibility, or Provocation

For decades, practitioners and scholars have argued over the correct criteria for judging scenarios. This is one of the most debated aspects of scenario building. Should we assess scenarios on their probability (how likely is each scenario to occur?), their plausibility (*could* each scenario happen?), or the degree to which they are provocative (do they create an emotional response?)? Once again, there is no correct selection, and there are many opinions in the field. One caution about using probability as the criterion: once a scenario is judged to be highly unlikely (or very low probability), it will tend to be dismissed. It is simply the way human cognition works: we pay attention to things we believe are likely to happen. This practice could actually defeat one of the general purposes of scenarios—to stretch and challenge the thinking. Remember, Shell's planning systems (before scenarios) were built on the assumption of predictability. Its planners found that their predictions were failing year after year, which was what led to the introduction of scenarios in the first place. Much has been written about and practiced around plausibility, particularly over the past decade (Ramirez & Selin, 2014). Plausibility allows for more flexibility in the judgment of scenarios and takes the process beyond either-or stances. Plausibility also challenges the scenario team to think more deeply about what *could* happen and puts the focus on truly novel, creative, and challenging scenarios. Provocation is also a tricky criterion to use because it too allows more flexibility in assessing scenarios. Most scenario planners would agree that if your scenarios do not get any kind of emotional reaction from participants, there is more work to be done. Put another way, if participants read scenarios and have no reaction, the scenarios have not done what they are supposed to do. Scenarios should challenge participants. Some may be depressing, others may be uplifting, and some have actually made people really angry.

I do not have advice here, though the caution with probability is strong enough that I do not use it or try to generate scenario likelihoods. In my experience, plausibility and provocation have been the most useful ways to judge the utility of scenarios. Perhaps some balance of the two is the optimal outcome. There is much more information available about these concepts, and the purpose of this section is not to review it all in depth. The purpose is to make you aware of other important issues in the scenario building process before we turn to the main point of this book—how to use them.

My standard approach to assessing scenarios is asking a subgroup of participants (maybe three to four) to read the scenarios and assess them on the following criteria:

1. Plausible—the scenarios have to be logically possible
2. Challenging—the scenario should provoke some kind of response. It should help you to see the possible future in a surprising way
3. Relevant—Each scenario should be relevant to the decisions on the table. The scenario (and the set) should be useful for thinking about potential decisions and actions
4. Factual—Finally, of course, if there is anything factually incorrect, it needs to be corrected

Summary and Implications

Of course, there are other approaches to building scenarios used by various futures studies schools, consulting firms, and independent scenario consultants. Some of them rely on computer models and

Bayesian statistical analysis, which are not covered in this chapter. It would probably be impossible to review all of the available methods for scenario building. The point of this chapter was only to highlight some of the most prevalent scenario building methods available in the practical domain, and to make it clear that different schools, philosophies, traditions, and practices have led to significant variety in how scenarios can be constructed. It is also important to acknowledge that this review has featured methods from the intuitive logics school of scenario planning. While I have included three methods entirely outside the intuitive logics school, there are many more, and any student of scenario planning would do well to explore the variety of methods beyond those I have mentioned here.

The implications of this chapter should be obvious. There are different ways to build scenarios. Some provide extensive freedom and choice, and some adhere to the 2 × 2 matrix method or a slight variation on it. And there are other methods quite unique in their approach that have a different basis and aim for different outcomes at the start. Scenario planning professionals have many options, and the degree of expertise and experience required to apply them varies according to any selected method and should be taken into account in the process of choosing a method. It is possible that after reading this book, you will have a much deeper understanding of different ways to use scenarios, which will inform the selection of the most appropriate scenario building method.

The methods that allow more freedom and flexibility require extensive experience in order to deal with the many choices involved. The premise of this book is that it really doesn't matter which method you use to build your scenarios. This tour was not intended to be fully comprehensive, as there are many different ways of thinking about scenarios that were not discussed here. The goal has been to review the most current, relevant, and influential scenario building methods.

The real pressure for scenario planners comes from the expectation that the scenarios will be used in ways that directly connect to benefits for the organization. Good scenario planning rests on a clearly articulated purpose, selection of a rigorous scenario building method, a capable or expert scenario facilitator, and using the scenarios in ways that achieve their purpose. The next chapter describes the transition from having scenarios to using scenarios. Seven different ways to use scenarios are briefly outlined as an introduction to the main contributions that come in the remaining chapters.

PART TWO

SPECIFIC WAYS TO USE SCENARIOS

4 ■ Seven Approaches to Using Scenarios

As a solution to the lack of existing guidance for using scenarios, the chapters in this section provide detailed descriptions of seven different ways to use scenarios:

1. Connecting scenarios to their original purposes
2. Generating strategies
3. Windtunneling strategies with scenarios
4. Testing decisions and options with scenarios
5. Estimating scenario financial benefits
6. Modeling scenario financials
7. Developing scenario signals and critical uncertainty dashboards

These different ways of using scenarios can be viewed as standalone exercises or can be combined in any way that fits. The encouragement is to use these tools and exercises in any way that is relevant to your situation. Do not try to force fit your situation into one of these chapters; rather, adapt these chapters, the suggestions, and the advice they contain to get the most out of your scenarios. You can view these chapters as a modular way of approaching how to use scenarios. Some of the approaches, exercises, and the descriptions they contain may be exactly what you are looking for. Others may be irrelevant. The point is to take what you can from what is provided. The advice these chapters contain is based on over two decades of research, application, trial and error, and refinement. They all work—if what you are trying to achieve is aligned with what is described. Even so, the world of practice and application is messy, and you should feel free to adjust these methods and be creative to meet your needs. Templates for working with scenarios in these seven ways are provided in each chapter and (in more usable formats) on my website (www.chermackscenarios.com).

1. Connecting Scenarios to the Original Purposes

Scenarios are developed for different purposes. At a high level, scenarios can be used simply to wonder about how the industry—or the world—could change in unexpected ways. They can also be used to assess a specific decision. Chapter 5 highlights the fact that every scenario project begins with a purpose in mind. Often it is not stated, which introduces ambiguity into the scenario work. It is very helpful to define a purpose at the start. This practice can align expectations and ensure that the scenario work will focus where it needs to. Since so few projects claim a clear purpose at the start, a good time to be deliberate about how to use scenarios is when you have completed a set of them, and this chapter shows you how. Chapter 5 guides you through different scenario purposes and provides clear advice for how to get back on track if the project lacks a clearly articulated purpose from the start.

2. Generating Strategies (Generic Strategies, Opportunities and Threats, and Adapting, Mitigating, and Thriving)

Chapter 6 focuses on how to generate high-level strategies for what actions could be taken if each scenario were to come true. It describes three different ways of using scenarios to develop these ideas: (1) generic strategies, (2) opportunities and threats, and (3) adapting, mitigating, and thriving. These exercises can be simple and nonspecific. For many decision makers, these exercises alone can bring value to the creation of scenarios. Further, these exercises can support creative thinking about what could become strategy, though further detail is required. Nonetheless, the exercises are intended for those who have scenarios and want to explore the future, not pin it down. Yet, the outcomes of these simple exercises can become inputs to later chapters that get more specific.

3. Windtunneling Strategies with Scenarios

Chapter 7 describes how to use scenarios to develop a strategic plan and then test it. The outputs from chapter 6 can be direct inputs to this work, or you can use an existing strategic plan. However, as we have already seen, most strategic plans are vague and do not provide the level of detail required to be useful. The difference between generating strategies (as described in chapter 6) and the specifics of creating a strategic plan is the level of detail required. To get to a strategic plan, the actions have to be specific and action oriented, and accompanying details like scope, schedule, budget, and timeline need to be clarified. Chapter 7 shows you how to take ideas and translate them into a practical, useful, and applicable strategic plan.

The second part of chapter 7 demonstrates how to "windtunnel" or stress-test a strategic plan. The main point is to check whether, how, and where the strategies fall apart. What is particularly useful about the exercises described in chapter 7 is that you will come away with a list of specific strategies aligned with each scenario, and a smaller subset of specific strategies that can advance your organization regardless of any scenario that begins to emerge in reality.

4. Testing Decisions and Options with Scenarios

Getting more specific, sometimes there is a critical decision with several possible options on the table. Chapter 8 describes how to use the scenarios to assess the potential benefits and risks associated with the options. Think of it as a more specific version of windtunneling. This use of scenarios is best for shorter-term timelines, and important near-term decisions are met with high levels of uncertainty. Two examples are provided and described with attention to the context, and descriptions of the decisions and related options. This is a specific exercise, and it requires that the decision be clearly defined and have comparable options.

5. Estimating Scenario Financial Benefits

Scenario planning does not usually involve any assessment or estimation of financial benefits for the project or the firm. This is one likely reason for the lack of full and long-term adoption in most companies. The purpose of chapter 9 is to present two ways of understanding and estimating the financial benefits of scenario work. When viewed as an intervention—just like leadership development or training—the outcomes of scenario planning can be quantified, estimated, and translated into financial gains or losses. Chapter 9 describes two approaches to assessing the utility of any scenario exercise: (1) Was the initial scenario planning intervention itself worth the time, investment, and other resources required? and (2) Did the scenario planning effort lead to later decisions that created a financial benefit? These questions reflect both short- and long-term timelines, and two strategies for answering these questions are described.

6. Modeling Scenario Financials

Modeling scenario financials requires creating a connection among scenarios, strategic planning, and the finance department (see chapter 10). Bringing these activities together is how a company can really gain the benefits of scenario planning. Because scenario planning is a strategic-level intervention, it should be clear that some of its benefits take time to realize. The point is to involve the finance team and let them consider the implications of each scenario for the overall financial performance of the company. While every company will have different ways of showing financial models, there are some basic elements that need to be considered. Common elements of a business model include an income statement, a balance sheet, and a cash-flow statement. These can be lengthy analyses, and chapter 10 describes a simplified way to consider the overall financial implications according to each scenario. These pieces can be estimated for each scenario. With some creative thinking (which finance teams are not necessarily known for), scenarios can provide the ability to consider the overall organizational position and how it will vary across the assumptions presented by the scenarios.

7. Developing Scenario Signals and Critical Uncertainty Dashboards

Signals are one of the most useful, and often overlooked, benefits of scenarios. They should be mandatory and are not necessarily a specific way of using scenarios. They are critically important in keeping the scenarios alive. Signals are the events required for a given scenario to appear in reality. They are usually written as newspaper headlines or short snippets that scroll across the bottom of your favorite news channel. In looking at any scenario, certain events are required in order to make it come true. Identifying the events required for each scenario to become reality has serious benefits. This activity creates a feedback loop with the external environment as time passes. While the goal is never that any one scenario "gets the future right," over time, the world will evolve more toward the events and descriptions of a single scenario over others. However, it is almost always a mix of the set of scenario dynamics.

Critical uncertainty dashboards are useful in specific situations. For example, the recent COVID-19 pandemic provoked a series of relatively short-term but highly uncertain sets of variables: How long would the pandemic last? What would be the availability of testing? How accurate would it be? What is the timeline for a potential vaccine? Will the vaccine candidates be successful? How long does

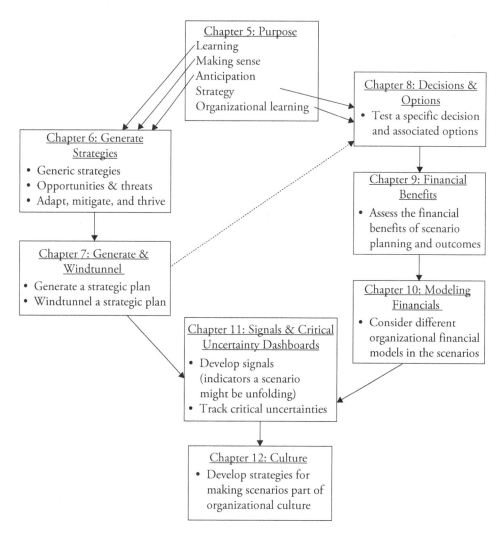

Figure 4.1. Overall Process Flow for Using Scenarios

immunity last? What is the accuracy and efficacy of antibody testing? What is the trajectory of cases—increasing or decreasing? Will the recommended public health measures be effective in reducing the number of cases?

Scenarios for crises that have already arrived are not very useful. Scenarios should focus on anticipating the next crisis. However, in the short term, under circumstances like COVID-19—when there is an extensive list of critical uncertainties—it can be useful to forgo scenarios and create a critical uncertainty dashboard. This is a simple tool that allows for the tracking of short-term developments and provides a way to assess the situation.

Chapter 11 describes the development of both signals and critical uncertainty dashboards. Further, it describes how to use them. The utility of these tools should not be overlooked as they are arguably some of the most practically useful ways to use scenarios. They should be mandatory.

Integrative Model

Again, these approaches can be used separately or in almost any modular combination. The outputs of some approaches can be logical inputs to others. It all depends on the purpose for developing scenarios and the level of detail sought for examining and testing various organizational decisions and issues. Figure 4.1 captures a suggested process flow through the seven approaches and a suggestion for how they could be combined in a longer-term scenario use process.

Summary

The chapters in this section are the focus of this book and are intended as an initial vaccine against the infections caused by the incomplete and problematic practices of strategic and scenario planning. These approaches are effective. The key is to understand the diagnosis and write an effective prescription for the given circumstances. These chapters can work together or be used individually according to the dynamics of the situation. In other words, all of the following activities can be used, adjusted, modified, or combined so as to begin the process of using scenarios and applying them. The intent is to move beyond simply creating scenarios as interesting thought exercises, which has held the field back for so long.

5 ■ Connecting Scenarios to Their Original Purposes

Scenarios should have a purpose. They can be general or specific and everything in between. Some scenarios are used simply to encourage creative thinking and wonder about the future, while others are focused on a specific situation or decision. Failure to articulate a purpose at the start is common in scenario planning. However, having an intended purpose connects directly to how the scenarios can be used. Most publicly available sets of scenarios do not include a stated project purpose, and even more fail to examine whether the purpose was achieved.

Take, for example, Shell's publicly available scenarios on its website (currently titled "Mountains," "Oceans," and "Sky" [https://www.shell.com/energy-and-innovation/the-energy-future/scenarios.html]). These are explorations of the energy industry. They are global in nature and are necessarily broad. While not stated, their purpose is to provoke learning and insights about the energy industry, to wonder about how the entire global industry could evolve and change in ways people might not be thinking about. Shell also has many smaller, more focused scenarios that are not publicly available. These scenarios outline regions of the world, specific exploration and development projects, investment decisions, and other more detailed aspects of organizational operations. These are decision scenarios, and their purpose is to inform decisions that leaders might consider.

It is impossible to talk about using scenarios without talking about their effectiveness. It is important to clarify a purpose and intent for scenario work even before it begins. Specifying a purpose helps keep the project on track, provides a basis for using scenarios, and allows for evaluating their utility and managing expectations (Chermack, 2017; Ramirez & Wilkinson, 2016). However, this is not a common practice. Even in cases that do not involve a clear purpose from the start, it is critical to reflect on why the project was initiated in the first place. What has been achieved? Did we generate important insights? Do we understand the external environment in a different way? Did the scenarios inform important decisions? What was the outcome?

This chapter describes several categories of scenario planning purpose in order to illustrate that scenarios must have a reason to be developed and used (Carter et al., 2001; Schnaars, 1987). Yes, there are leaders who simply want to use scenarios to check their thinking—what are we not thinking about? And there are others who want to test a specific investment decision and consider the implications. These are entirely different purposes. Until now, these purposes have not been specifically and practically outlined for anyone who wants to use scenarios.

Learning Scenarios and Decision Scenarios

Scenarios can generally be divided into two categories: learning scenarios and decision scenarios (Wack, 1984). The differentiation is based on two possible high-level initial purposes—either to learn or to make decisions.

According to Wack, "Scenarios explore for facts out there, but they aim at perceptions inside the head of critical decision makers.

Their purpose is to gather and transform information of potential strategic significance into fresh perceptions that then lead to strategic insights that were previously beyond the mind's reach—those that would not even have been considered" (1985a, p. 88). Because Shell is the most prominent organization with the longest history of consistent scenario use and continued experimentation and evolution, it can offer important insights.

Learning Scenarios

Throughout the early development of scenarios at Shell, the teams began with higher-level, global learning scenarios—how could the industry change in unexpected ways? (Chermack, 2011, 2017; Wilkinson & Kupers, 2013, 2014). The early scenarios allowed for insights and a way of seeing the industry landscape much more broadly. They also supported the idea that much of the scenario process involves learning to re-perceive one's own assumptions, to expand the thought process. Stated simply, the purpose of using learning scenarios is not to take action but to generate learning and insight (Wack, 1984). These scenarios provoke a sense of wonder about the future, typically have longer timelines (sometimes 20–50 years), and are an essential part of taking a truly long view. However, because these scenarios are not action oriented, project sponsors often react with a feeling of "so what?" As a result, the purpose of this book and particularly this chapter becomes clear. It is important to clarify and understand precisely the purpose of any scenario effort and how it is intended to be used. There are times when thinking the unthinkable, simply asking "what if?," or trying to expose stuck mental models or assumptions is an appropriate and powerful use of scenarios.

Decision Scenarios

Over several years, the scenario teams at Shell began to realize there was another, more focused approach to scenarios. These became known as decision scenarios (Wack, 1984, 1985a). Here the purpose was much more specific: to inform a particular decision. To drill off the coast of Siberia? To stop the purchase of oil tankers? These specific projects required scenarios that were much more focused on the issue, and the intent was to use the scenarios to test how a given decision and investment would play out in the shorter term in a few different futures. Indeed, Shell's scenario teams created a hierarchy of scenarios, with learning scenarios framing the industry-level view and specific decision scenarios at regional or decision-level problems (Wack, 1985a).

A Metaphor

A camera lens can be a useful metaphor. Learning scenarios are like the panoramic feature: you can see a wide scene, but the details are missing. Decision scenarios are like the close-up feature: extreme details are shown, but the background is often blurred. And then there is everything in between, which can be achieved by zooming in or out. This is the space of difficult and customized scenario work. No matter what the zoom setting might be, there is always a purpose behind the photographer's image, just as there should be with scenarios.

Van der Heijden's Categories of Scenario Purpose

Another categorization of scenario purposes provides more insight and further detail (van der Heijden, 2004). In a seminal paper in 2004, van der Heijden describes a specific categorization of scenario planning purposes (figure 5.1). By considering the distinction between content and process, and thinking and action, four specific ways of thinking about scenario purpose are gained.

Van der Heijden was a successor to Pierre Wack at Shell, and, in fact, he spent several years under the tutelage of Wack in order to document what was learned at Shell over Wack's 20 years as a leader of scenario planning (Chermack, 2017). Van der Heijden went on to helm the scenario team from 1989 to 1991. His contributions to scenario planning have been significant, with several books and a long list of articles.

Understanding figure 5.1 requires some explanation. Consider the two axes van der Heijden used: thinking versus action, and

	Content one-off	**Process** ongoing
Thinking opening up	*Making sense*	*Anticipation*
Action closure	*Optimal strategy*	*Adaptive learning*

Figure 5.1. Van der Heijden's Categories of Scenario Purpose (2004)

content versus process. These are useful differentiators when thinking about scenario planning. Is the purpose to think differently about a situation or to make a decision and take action? Is the effort a specific, single application, or is the goal to make scenario thinking an ongoing part of organizational decision making? At the outset, these are important aspects of scenario planning.

Combining these two aspects of scenario purpose (once again, in a matrix) allows for the ability to refine what the scenario effort is supposed to produce in terms of outcomes. It is helpful, then, to consider each quadrant of the matrix.

One-Off Content + Opening Up Thinking: Making Sense
Scenario work in this category is focused on understanding confusing trends in the environment. There are often aspects of the external environment that require more detailed study with a goal of deeper understanding. The flurry of COVID-19 scenarios from March 2020 to June 2020 available on the internet were representative of this category. The goal—as the quadrant is labeled—is to make sense of the environment and the dynamics that can signal change. Scenario projects of regional economic performance,

general climate environments, and individual mobility in specific regions, among other general trends, are in this category.

The vast majority of scenario work is in this category. Decision makers often want a quick solution, and nowhere has this been more evident than in the COVID-19 pandemic. There was extensive scenario work aimed at projecting different ways the virus could evolve in the short term.

When decision makers want a new process they hope will solve an immediate problem, odds are that they are already too late. Many instances of scenario work have resulted in an ultimate judgment that results in disappointment with the outcomes. This is the danger of scenarios in this category. Defining a purpose clarifies the expected outcomes and ensures that participants and stakeholders are in agreement about the goal they are trying to achieve.

What to do about this? This chapter addresses this issue, and it reflects the importance of having a clear intent at the start of any scenario effort. Much can be learned from the leading organizations that have used scenarios for decades. You can look at Shell Oil, Anglo American, and General Electric, among many others. The lesson is that rarely have one-off scenario exercises, intended to solve a pertinent immediate problem, been successful and led to sustained forward thinking about the future.

Ongoing Process + Opening Up Thinking: Anticipation

There are extensive examples of scenarios being used to create an ongoing forum for creative thinking without a specific decision or initiative in mind (Gordon, 2020; Kahane, 2012; Schoemaker, 2020). In many cases, the intent is to create a shared understanding of possible changes in the external business environment over time. This approach can be helpful in building a common view and developing alignment. This quadrant in van der Heijden's matrix is labeled "anticipation." Continually using scenarios as a wide-ranging radar allows for the ability to react faster than competitors. However, the key is that scenarios have to become institutionalized and reviewed as ongoing work.

To achieve this, scenarios should be a part of annual strategic planning and annual business planning and should be used in any case of a serious investment decision. To do less is to neglect the external environment. For example, at Shell, managers with budget responsibility are required to justify their investment decisions by demonstrating their performance across a set of scenarios. Requiring the use of scenarios as part of the organizational decision-making process is critical to institutionalizing scenarios. According to van der Heijden (2004), cases of ongoing scenario planning show the ability to balance between strategic fragmentation across the organization and groupthink. In other words, embedding scenarios as a standard organizational process addresses two common problems in organizational strategy.

Of particular importance in this category are signals (Mendonça et al., 2004; Schoemaker et al., 2013), sometimes referred to as signposts. Signals are events that are required for any given scenario to unfold. When done well, signals allow scenario users to keep track of changes in the external environment. As they build up over time, signals have the potential to indicate that the world may be evolving more like one scenario than the others. Signals are covered in depth in a later chapter with complete guidelines.

One-Off Content + Action Closure: Optimal Strategy

In the lower-left box, titled "Optimal strategy," the goal is to develop a specific preferred strategy. This is probably the most common initial purpose for scenario planning: decision makers want help in a specific context with a specific strategy in mind. This is also where the most failures occur—trying a new process or tool with the hopes it might be a silver bullet and assist in a time of serious decision-making pressure for a high-risk situation. There are certainly instances in which this is useful (more on that later), and the most common mistake is to "try out" scenario planning without having made the purpose explicit. It is rare that a single instance of scenario planning can produce truly insightful strategy options. "Generally we have come to the conclusion that stand-alone scenario projects aiming for a deliverable of a specific optimal strategy are difficult to turn into a success" (van der Heijden, 2004, p. 157).

Ongoing Content + Action Closure: Adaptive Learning

This category of scenario work is focused on the ongoing use of scenarios as part of a larger strategy system. The goal is to engage in ongoing organizational learning based on action. In these cases, scenarios are designed to provoke action—for example, new actions, new markets, and new partnerships. The previous categories of purpose can all be thought of as steps toward arriving at this one. The ultimate payback of investing in scenarios is in taking action and incorporating the results into an ongoing organizational learning feedback loop (van der Heijden, 2004).

Focusing Question

Scenario work always needs a starting point. Because scenarios focus on the external environment, focusing questions are necessarily general. Focusing questions should be targeted at how the environment could change. Remember that scenarios have to describe the external world in new and provocative ways. It is important to realize that the purpose of the project and the focusing question are different things, though they are necessarily related. A standard scenario focusing question is the following:

> How could the external environment for *x* organization evolve and change over the next *x* years?

Articulating the purpose of the scenario effort at the start is crucial. The question "How do we intend to use the scenarios and what do we hope to get out of the process?" should be asked and answered in the beginning stages of the project. This is no different than any other investment of organizational resources. If there is no attention to what the expected outcomes might be, the scenario process is not likely to produce useful outcomes. However, if there are even vague ideas of the purpose and expectations, it is easy to check on what was actually achieved compared with what the intended outputs were. Because this simple definition is so often overlooked, another natural point in the overall scenario process is to consider (or reconsider) the purpose when you have completed your scenario building.

Workshop Format and Guidelines: Determine and/or Clarify the Scenario Purpose

Time: 2 hours.
Participants: 5–15.

Assumptions: You have a set of scenarios and you may or may not have defined a purpose.

Workshop Format: Whether a purpose was specified at the start of your scenario work or not, this activity forces the conversation of why scenarios were developed at all and what they are intended to be used for. Assemble the scenario team and consider the following questions:

Instructions:

- If an initial purpose was intended for developing scenarios, have we achieved it?
- If there was no initial purpose, what do we want to do with the scenarios now?
  - It can be helpful to start with Wack's two general categories: learning scenarios and decision scenarios. Which category captures the intent of how we will use our scenarios? To be more specific, consider van der Heijden's categories of purpose:
    - Is the goal to make sense of an uncertain situation?
    - Is the goal to be able to anticipate changes in the environment?
    - Is the goal to develop a direct input to strategy making?
    - Is the goal to create or sustain an adaptive organizational learning system?
- This exercise can simply be a conversation, though someone should capture a record of it.
- Notes from the meeting should be compiled, distributed, and circulated, and members of the team should be asked to provide any additional ideas.

- Depending on the outcomes, next steps could be to summarize what was generally learned or to consider the more detailed tools in the rest of this book to achieve the desired outcomes.

Summary

Using the workshop activity provides a way to understand and gain clarity around the general purpose (or purposes) of the scenario exercise. Having spent time and energy on developing scenarios, it is vital to revisit why the investment of time and energy was made. Because it is uncommon that a specific purpose is identified at the start of most scenario planning exercises, it is a good time to pause and think more deeply about outcomes and expectations. Following the advice provided in this chapter can direct you and your team to other activities in the coming chapters.

The point of this chapter is to make it clear that scenarios need a purpose, an intention, and a reason to be made. That reason really should be clearly articulated at the start of the project, which often does not happen. In these cases, it is certainly useful to ask the question, Why did we decide to develop scenarios in the first place? And to follow on, What did we get out of this work? Even retrospectively, it is helpful to ask, Did we learn something new? Did we identify options we couldn't see before? Did the scenarios help us with our decision making? Once you have developed your scenarios is a good time to reconsider how they should be used and which strategies make the most sense to achieve the original purpose. This chapter provides a necessary starting point for understanding how you want to use your scenarios and for what purpose.

6 ▪ Generating Strategies

Once scenarios have been built, the next objective is to understand what can be done to take advantage of the possible changes in the external environment that they highlight. It does not matter what process or method was used to develop the scenarios. When scenarios are used to create a path into the future, they can be helpful in exploring new possibilities (Favato & Vecchiato, 2017). In these cases, specific decisions are not usually on the table. The goal is to identify different ways of thinking and potential options that were not seen prior to building scenarios. One way to go about this is to use scenarios to identify generic, high-level strategies for each scenario. A second is to consider the opportunities and threats that each scenario presents. Yet another way is to consider how to adapt to each of the scenarios, how to mitigate their potential negative effects, and how to thrive in the context of what each future might bring. The challenge is to find strategies that can succeed in a variety of conditions.

This chapter describes three ways of using scenarios to generate strategies: (1) generic strategies, (2) opportunities and threats, and (3) adapting, mitigating, and thriving. These three activities are useful in preparing decision makers for possible courses of action as well as when they might take them. The exercises described in this chapter are relatively simple, and they are often used to initiate a strategic conversation (Ramirez & Wilkinson, 2016; van der Heijden, 2011). These exercises are most relevant when the scenarios are intended to make sense of the external environment. This chapter is a good starting point for those who have developed scenarios and simply want to use them to think about the future and consider how scenarios may change their understanding of what is possible—they connect to a purpose of exploration and learning rather than decision making.

The specific assumption underneath these exercises is that decision makers have not yet defined a set of decisions and options (Wright & Goodwin, 1999). They want to use the scenarios to explore the future and think about what could change. The purpose is to use the insights gained from the scenario building work to consider new ideas and possible strategies. These exercises can be applied in sequence, or any combination or single approach can be used as is relevant to the situation.

Generic Strategies

The simplest approach to using scenarios is to think about what generic strategies might be available under the conditions of each scenario. The basic question is, What would we do now if we knew this scenario was going to come true? The question is repeated for each scenario. It doesn't matter if you have two, three, or four or more scenarios. Scenario participants are asked to consider the question, and using scenarios has begun (Asher & Lascarides, 2013; van der Heijden, 2005). The point is not to be overly detailed in this activity; there are more detailed approaches to using scenarios in later chapters. Instead, it is to start engaging with what the scenarios might mean for the organization at a very high level. This is

Scenario A   Critical Uncertainty 1   Scenario B

- Generic strategy 1   - Generic strategy 1
- Generic strategy 2   - Generic strategy 2
- Generic strategy 3   - Generic strategy 3
- Generic strategy 4   - Generic strategy 4
- Etc.   - Etc.

Critical Uncertainty 2

- Generic strategy 1   - Generic strategy 1
- Generic strategy 2   - Generic strategy 2
- Generic strategy 3   - Generic strategy 3
- Generic strategy 4   - Generic strategy 4
- Etc.   - Etc.

Scenario D   Scenario C

Figure 6.1. Scenarios and Generic Strategies Template

	Scenario 1	Scenario 2	Scenario 3
Strategies	• Generic strategy	• Generic strategy	• Generic strategy
	• Generic strategy	• Generic strategy	• Generic strategy
	• Etc.	• Etc.	• Etc.

Figure 6.2. Modified Scenarios and Generic Strategies Template

more like a brainstorming activity, though it is within the boundaries of each scenario.

The approach can be applied directly in the 2 × 2 scenario matrix (if one is used in the scenario building process) or in any other scenario structure (see figure 6.1).

If the scenario building process does not use the 2 × 2 matrix approach, the template can be modified as in figure 6.2.

Example: Fish and Wildlife Agency

A scenario planning project with Fish and Wildlife Agency focused on how the agency could manage the changing public views of wildlife and the related implications. Across the United States, sales of hunting and fishing licenses—a significant source of revenue for the agency—are declining. Scenario planning was used to understand how the future environment for Fish and Wildlife Agency could change. Four scenarios were built, and participants were asked to read scenario 1 and comment on generic strategies for the agency in that scenario. The process was repeated for the other three scenarios. Figure 6.3 provides an example of the generic strategies exercise for Fish and Wildlife Agency.

The outcome of this scenario exercise was to provide Fish and Wildlife Agency with general strategies that map to each scenario and to determine whether there were high-level strategies that were helpful across the set of scenarios. What follows is a description of exactly how the generic strategies workshop was facilitated, with the intent to provide enough detail that you could apply this yourself.

Workshop Format and Guidelines: Generic Strategies

Time: 2 hours.
Participants: 5–15.

Assumptions: You have a set of scenarios.

Workshop Format: The purpose of this workshop is to create high-level potential generic strategies for each scenario.

Instructions:

- Participants read scenario 1 and individually consider the question, What would we do now if we knew this scenario was going to come true?
- The facilitator notes the generic strategies from each participant on a white board, projected computer screen, online platform, or other.
- Participants talk about the generic strategies and debate them.

Social Values—Toward Mutualist	
- Technical assistance to improve quality of habitat in and near urban areas - Influence development codes to be wildlife habitat friendly - Shift Wildlife Recreation Program from urban/suburban fee/ce acquisitions - Partner with commerce, science centers, zoos - Target new residents and meet them where they are - Offer wildlife viewing expeditions - Create urban habitat spaces with corridors - Reprioritize focus (acquisition) on urban habitats - Shift existing Department of Fish and Wildlife staff capacity toward nongame while increasing reliance on comanagement of game space with tribes - Identify new revenue sources (i.e., Coke using wildlife spaces for royalties to DFW) - DFW-owned transportation to get urban folks out to "Big nature" (DFW lands) - Biologists become nature guides and can charge for participating in experiences	- Consider culling deer and elk to avoid wild fluctuations in populations of deer and elk and carnivores and/or contaminants of disease - Staff shifted toward zoonotic disease unit - Emergency declaration for open access to new funds - Increase restoration of sea grasses: kelp to store carbon (trade-off in ecosystem) - Monitor base of food web and acidification to prioritize areas and actions to identify at-risk areas - Work with superintendent of public schools to integrate at-risk wildlife education into statewide curriculum - Increase health testing - Partner with health and food industry - Disease mitigation and emergency management - Enhance emergency management - Science around disease statistics to help plants and animals adapt to acidifications - Are there ways to protect and preserve endangered species from natural disaster?

Figure 6.3. Generic Strategies for Fish and Wildlife Agency

Habitat—Urban	Habitat—Wild
- Green energy development codes and mitigation methods - Work with ranching/farming community to preserve native habitat - Enhance emergency management processes (east vs. west tensions) - Partner with tech company leaders to innovate around solar and wildlife conflicts - More outreach and education around ranching and farming practices - Enhanced and tailored messaging - Work with farmers to develop wildlife-friendly practices in addition to incentives to conserve shrub steppe (state farm bill and funding) - Fund community gardens - Incentivize solar development in urban areas - Wildlife-friendly solar best management practices	- Develop community-based grant programs to further enhance pace and effectiveness of coexistence efforts - Try to outpace climate impact on people and wildlife - Work with Office of Superintendent of Public Instruction to integrate living with wildlife into statewide school curriculum - Harness community programs to advocate for fish and wildlife protections in renewable energy regulation - Reconsider the positive effects of hydro energy/h2o storage in light of water supply challenges - Identify costs and impact of green energy and make green greener - Provide outreach for what responsible watching and living with wildlife looks like, using conservation corps - Learn how to better recycle water for fish production/health and public education
Social Values—Divisive	

Figure 6.3. (continued)

- Repeat this process for each scenario.
- When generic strategies have been generated for all scenarios, consolidate the duplications.
- Focus on developing strategies for each scenario and finding the common generic strategies across all scenarios.

Products

- Generic strategies identified for each scenario
- Generic strategies identified across the set of scenarios

Opportunities and Threats

Another easy way to use scenarios to think about strategies is for the team to consider the opportunities and threats that each scenario presents. The activity can reveal options that were not previously considered, and lead to more rigorous thinking. The goal is to think about how to take advantage of the opportunities and how to prepare for (or avoid) the threats.

The starting point of this activity is to be aware that each scenario will present unique potential opportunities and threats. The scenario team should have the necessary expertise to identify and describe them, along with strategies that either take advantage of opportunities or compensate for threats. The template in figure 6.4 provides a structure for organizing this exercise.

Scenario	Opportunities	Strategies	Threats	Strategies
Scenario 1				
Scenario 2				
Scenario 3				
Scenario 4				

Figure 6.4. Scenario Opportunities and Threats Template

Example: Healthcare Company

A scenario project with Healthcare Company in the United States focused on the changing nature, demographics, disease, and other uncertainties that could dramatically affect the industry and the business portfolio. Scenarios were built that aimed to stretch the thinking of leadership in terms of dramatic shifts that could pose significant opportunities and threats in the emerging external environment. Once the scenarios were completed, the leadership team was led through the opportunities and threats workshop; the results are shown in figure 6.5.

The outcome of this scenario work was intended to identify and describe the major opportunities and threats that each scenario contained and what could be done about them.

Workshop Format and Guidelines: Opportunities and Threats

Time: 3 hours.
Participants: 5–15.

Assumptions: You have a set of scenarios.

Workshop Format: The purpose of this workshop is to identify the major opportunities and threats, along with corresponding potential strategies for each scenario.

Instructions:

- Participants read scenario 1 and individually consider these two questions: What are the major opportunities and threats contained in this scenario? How would we take advantage of the opportunities and minimize or avoid the threats?
- Participants note their responses on the template provided in figure 6.4, and when complete, report their views.
- The facilitator notes the opportunities and threats from each participant on a white board, projected computer screen, online platform, or other.

Scenario	Opportunities	Strategies	Threats	Strategies
Scenario 1	Desperate need for health-care support, but government structures prohibit success Cures for cancer, blindness, obesity	Lobbying efforts—increased attention to our relationships with state governments Opportunity to track developments in these areas and be on the leading edge of the cures	Health care takes a backseat to larger global issues Political unrest and upheaval Major divide between haves and have-nots	We are in a slump, focus on internal efficiencies Consider how to cut costs to make medications and procedures more affordable
Scenario 2	Personal technology advancements Available disposable income and a focus on health care	Ramp up our own understanding and investment on the tech side Consider a few innovation projects and products that may be expensive but that people would be able to afford	Complicated access systems Reimbursements dysfunctional Increased scrutiny from regulators	Streamline our own access systems Can we get involved in / overtake the reimbursement process?

Figure 6.5. Healthcare Company Opportunities and Threats Example

Scenario	Opportunities	Strategies	Threats	Strategies
Scenario 3	Numerous potential diseases develop

Significant medical technology advancement | Many of our innovations in process could help—keep investing in these

Maintain or increase our investments in medical technologies— we are already on the edge of innovation | Economic and environmental crises create migration

Disease spreads quickly

Collapsing economies pose real threat | How do we aim for low-cost solutions?

Tracking migration allows our ability to focus efforts in certain states / regions |
| Scenario 4 | Leveraging social media more effectively to inform and persuade consumers

Pharmaceutical cure for diabetes pioneered | Do we even have a social media presence? We probably should . . .

Ramp up diabetes research and products—we have some, but this scenario suggests real opportunities | Dichotomous: economy recovered but consumers anxious

Booming economy results in major deregulation of industry | Marketing and trust building with the public is critical

Innovative and higher-cost products will be affordable, though probably to the "few." What are our ethics on this? |

Figure 6.5. (continued)

- The facilitator notes the suggested strategies for taking advantage of the opportunities and minimizing the threats.
- Participants talk about the outputs and debate them.
- Repeat this process for each scenario.
- When the process is complete for all scenarios, consolidate the duplications.
- Find the common strategies for capitalizing on the opportunities and avoiding the threats.

Products:

- Opportunities and threats identified for each scenario
- Strategies for taking advantage of the opportunities and avoiding the threats identified for each scenario
- Opportunities and threats that are common across the scenarios are identified
- Strategies for taking advantage of the opportunities and avoiding the threats across the scenarios are identified

Adapt, Mitigate, and Thrive

This approach follows the same general idea as the opportunities and threats workshop, though the goals are different. This approach has three targets:

1. Identify how the organization could adapt to each scenario (what changes might be needed in organizational structure, supply chain, culture, or products and services)
2. Identify how the organization might be able to mitigate the negative effects of each scenario (what actions could be taken to pivot)
3. Identify what would be required in order for the organization to thrive in each scenario context (see figure 6.6).

Example: Online University

The scenario work with Online University was based on a growing interest in online education at a large western public university in the United States. At the time, online courses and degrees were growing,

Scenario	Adapt	Mitigate	Thrive
Scenario 1			
Scenario 2			
Scenario 3			
Scenario 4			

Figure 6.6. Scenario Adapt, Mitigate, and Thrive Template

and the focusing question was just how fast they might continue to grow. Four scenarios were built and participants were asked to describe how to adapt to the scenario, how to mitigate the problems in the scenario, and how to thrive in the scenario. The process was repeated for the remaining three scenarios; the compiled results are provided in figure 6.7.

Workshop Format and Guidelines: Adapt, Mitigate, and Thrive

Time: 3 hours.
Participants: 5–15.

Assumptions: You have a set of scenarios.

Workshop Format: The purpose of this workshop is to identify potential ways the organization could adapt to each scenario, mitigate the problems in each scenario, and thrive in each scenario.

Instructions:

- Participants read scenario 1 and individually consider the following questions: What would we need to do to adapt to this scenario? What would we need to do to mitigate the problems in this scenario? and What would we need to do to thrive in this scenario?
- Participants fill out their own adapt, mitigate, thrive worksheet.
- The facilitator records responses in each category on a whiteboard, projected computer screen, online platform, or other.

Scenario	Adapt	Mitigate	Thrive
Single-Speed Bike Scenario	Get on faculty council and university curriculum commitee	Prioritize campus communications and building understanding, not just relationships	Continue investments in online conversion (moderately)
	Be transparent about money—invest wisely in university services	Keep quality	Marketing across the university to programs that might want online programs—services we can provide
	Define what success looks like for each unit and/or program	Advocate to the right individuals	
	Establish goals for success, knowing when university will help or hinder	Internal marketing—telling our story	
	Don't fight the battles	Get full buy-in on any external partnership	
	Articulate the value of continuing education for the community	Implement and clarify who we are to build our relationships	
	Advocate, advocate, advocate (externally)	Retention and growth go hand in hand	
	Define what we are good at, and excel regardless of support		

Figure 6.7. Online University's Adapt, Mitigate, and Thrive Strategies

Scenario	Adapt	Mitigate	Thrive
Cruiser Bike Scenario	How can we increase supply/capacity by partnering to fund faculty lines We're in a position to leverage quality and choose whether to aim for greater growth Disciplined teaching methods and services innovation Build a national reputation for excellence Select the few departments that support growth and focus resources there Expand by consulting and selling knowledge and experience related to quality and technology—will bring in more innovative staff to do this Select the few departments that support growth and focus resources there	Be aware of our spending nature Articulate Division of Continuing Education role and value to university leaders and stakeholders Prioritize internal communication to ensure there is not confusion about mission and vision Be more aware of maintaining opportunities for growth and development for staff to retain them Be more visible through community participation Articulate DCE role and value to university leaders and stakeholders If innovation is not a driver, focus on our partnership / our value Focus on methods and services, not technology innovation	Promote hiring of faculty—every way we can Build programs online with excellence in mind (created by tenure / tenure track faculty)

Figure 6.7. (continued)

Scenario	Adapt	Mitigate	Thrive
Cannondale Bike Scenario	Internal roles and communication Need to resource infrastructure / cross-training Retention plan Monitor data and quality Integrate into all department meetings—program team knows department inside and out Very large team / organizational structure needs to be tight—4 layers deep Internal roles and communication Advocate for quality in customer service and program development / management Define resident instruction success and its relationship to Division of Continuing Education success	Challenges presented by this scenario are easy to overcome Invest in staff, hiring, leadership, and HR development Invest in quality customer service— hire specifically at the customer service level	Hire, hire, hire! Develop programs— actively seek programs that want an online presence Support marketing to reach across the university to find the right programs

Figure 6.7. (continued)

Scenario	Adapt	Mitigate	Thrive
Banana-Seat Bike Scenario	Rebuild, restructure, and refocus on a few programs Establish priorities for specific efforts in program growth and quality Focus on external reputation and quality Prove we are a better choice than going alone (lost quality) Define directed strategies around student and program achievements Define what we would do if registration was not a service we offer Maintain the core values of the customer experience statement	Keep our positive results visible to administration and use data to drive decisions Stay conservative / aware of spending, even when funds are abundant Invest to keep the student as the customer, not the supplier as customer	Choose boutique programs—those ripe for online transition Focus groups with students from selected programs—what do they want?

Figure 6.7. (continued)

- Participants are invited to talk about the outputs and debate them.
- Repeat this process for each scenario.
- When the process is complete for all scenarios, consolidate the duplications.
- Identify specific actions for each scenario and analyze what is common across the scenarios.

Products:

- Strategies for adapting to each scenario
- Strategies for mitigating the challenges in each scenario
- Strategies for thriving in each scenario
- Strategies for adapting, mitigating, and thriving that are common across the set of scenarios

Summary

The exercises described in this chapter are generally qualitative in nature, meaning that they are intended to begin the process of using scenarios. These are first steps in using scenarios. They are simple exercises and do not require specific performance measures or financial estimates, and they can be completed in a short amount of time. While they are simple, when thinking about cases in which the scenarios are not used at all, or there is no specific guidance on what to do with them, these exercises can be powerful.

These approaches are most useful when there is not a specific direction, decision, or set of options already defined. The outputs of these exercises are usually bulleted lists of ideas that could be useful in further integrating scenarios and strategy, and they are focused on using scenarios to learn and make sense of the external environment (Chermack, 2017; van der Heijden, 2005; Wack, 1985b). The outputs of all these exercises can be taken further into the processes, tools, and guidance in the chapters that follow. Chapter 7 will show you how to use these outputs to build a strategic plan and test it.

7 ■ Windtunneling Strategies with Scenarios

Generating strategies is the first and most obvious way to use scenarios. The ideas presented in chapter 6 showed three different ways to generate strategies. The next step is to assess how those strategies hold up in each scenario and across the set of scenarios. The purpose of this chapter is to describe the concept of windtunneling and show you how to use it to test your strategies. This chapter will describe the concept of windtunneling, show an example of windtunneling strategies through scenarios, and explain how to adjust the outcomes of windtunneling to make them more precise and detailed for strategic planning. The results of these activities will help you determine a set of strategies that are useful across the set of scenarios, and add more clarity so that they are truly actionable.

Windtunneling

Windtunneling is the process of using scenarios to test strategies or possible actions (Chermack, 2011; de Ruijter, 2014; van der Heijden, 2011; Wade, 2012). When engineers create a new car or airplane, it is a common practice to put the structure in a wind tunnel and observe, for example, under what conditions the wings start to fall apart. The purpose of this is to determine airflow and ultimately to understand the structural integrity of the object being windtunneled. The concept is the same with scenario planning, except instead of windtunneling structures you are windtunneling ideas. To go a step further, scenarios provide multiple wind tunnels based on the idea that you cannot predict the environment in which you may need to operate. Instead of just a single variable (e.g., wind speed), scenarios allow you to test potential ideas and strategies in multiple future environments.

Other authors mention windtunneling as a way to use scenarios (e.g., de Ruijter, 2014; van der Heijden, 2011), though again the available guidance is not clear enough to apply. It is possible to windtunnel just about anything, and the overall process is the same. While this chapter focuses specifically on windtunneling strategies, you can windtunnel organizational culture, workforce capacity, and organization structure, among many other things. Questions like, What kind of organizational culture would we need to perform in each of these scenarios? What kind of human resources, expertise, and capacity would we need to be successful in each of these scenarios? and What kind of organizational structure would we need to deliver our products or services in each of these scenarios? are often provoked through the scenario building process. The process of windtunneling can help to explore and answer these kinds of questions in a strategic way. The goal is to check how well a set of strategies can perform in a variety of future environments.

Windtunneling involves reviewing scenario 1, getting mentally absorbed in the dynamics of the scenario, and then asking how each strategy would perform in that scenario. The activity is repeated for the remaining scenarios. Figure 7.1 provides a generic windtunneling template.

Strategy	Scenario 1	Scenario 2	Scenario 3	Scenario 4
Strategy 1				
Strategy 2				
Strategy 3				
Strategy . . .				

Figure 7.1. Windtunneling Template

Example: Fish and Wildlife Agency

Using the Fish and Wildlife Agency example, the process for getting to windtunneling was as follows:

- Use the generic strategies workshop from chapter 6
- Clarify the common generic strategies across the set of scenarios

The outcomes of the generic strategies exercise are in figure 7.2, placed within the scenario matrix. Remember that these ideas are the outcomes of asking participants to consider the question, What would we do now if we knew this scenario was going to come true? The exercise was repeated for each of the four scenarios according to the instructions in chapter 6, and the outcome strategies are shown in figure 7.2.

As you can see, the matrix contains too many strategies to work with. The next step in thinking about windtunneling is to consolidate the ideas for each scenario into what is common across all of them. In other words, the goal is to find a common and manageable set of strategies that are helpful in all or most scenarios. In the case of Fish and Wildlife Agency, participants were asked to clarify and consolidate their ideas, looking for generic strategies across the set of scenarios. The resulting list of the most common and helpful strategies was as follows:

1. Develop targeted outreach to new [state] residents
2. Explore and identify new revenue sources (taxes, royalties, fees)

Social Values—Toward Mutualist	
- Technical assistance to improve quality of habitat in and near urban areas	- Consider culling deer and elk to avoid wild fluctuations in populations of deer and elk and carnivores and/or contaminants of disease
- Influence development codes to be wildlife habitat friendly	
- Shift Wildlife Recreation Program from urban/suburban fee/ce acquisitions	- Staff shifted toward zoonotic disease unit
- Partner with commerce, science centers, zoos	- Emergency declaration for open access to new funds
- Target new residents and meet them where they are	- Increase restoration of sea grasses: kelp to store carbon (trade-off in ecosystem)
- Offer wildlife viewing expeditions	
- Create urban habitat spaces with corridors	- Monitor base of food web and acidification to prioritize areas and actions to identify at-risk areas
- Reprioritize focus (acquisition) on urban habitats	
- Shift existing Department of Fish and Wildlife staff capacity toward nongame while increasing reliance on comanagement of game space with tribes	- Work with superintendent of public schools to integrate at-risk wildlife education into statewide curriculum
	- Increase health testing
- Identify new revenue sources (i.e., Coke using wildlife spaces for royalties to DFW)	- Partner with health and food industry
	- Disease mitigation and emergency management
- DFW-owned transportation to get urban folks out to "Big nature" (DFW lands)	- Enhance emergency management
	- Science around disease statistics to help plants and animals adapt to acidifications
- Biologists become nature guides and can charge for participating in experiences	- Are there ways to protect and preserve endangered species from natural disaster?

Figure 7.2. Generic Strategies for Fish and Wildlife Agency

Habitat—Urban	Habitat—Wild
- Green energy development codes and mitigation methods - Work with ranching/farming community to preserve native habitat - Enhance emergency management processes (east vs. west tensions) - Partner with tech company leaders to innovate around solar and wildlife conflicts - More outreach and education around ranching and farming practices - Enhanced and tailored messaging - Work with farmers to develop wildlife-friendly practices in addition to incentives to conserve shrub steppe (state farm bill and funding) - Fund community gardens - Incentivize solar development in urban areas - Wildlife-friendly solar best management practices	- Develop community-based grant programs to further enhance pace and effectiveness of coexistence efforts - Try to outpace climate impact on people and wildlife - Work with Office of Superintendent of Public Instruction to integrate living with wildlife into statewide school curriculum - Harness community programs to advocate for fish and wildlife protections in renewable energy regulation - Reconsider the positive effects of hydro energy/h2o storage in light of water supply challenges - Identify costs and impact of green energy and make green greener - Provide outreach for what responsible watching and living with wildlife looks like, using conservation corps - Learn how to better recycle water for fish production/health and public education
Social Values—Divisive	

Figure 7.2. (continued)

3. Increase partnerships with public, private, and nongovernmental organizations
4. Partner with education to enhance K–12 wildlife curriculum
5. Offer "see and experience" wildlife tours
6. Restructure Fish and Wildlife Agency to regional offices
7. Develop and provide resources for enhanced emergency management planning
8. Engage partners and facilitate discussions on at-risk ecosystems
9. Invest in climate change analysis tools and programs
10. Modify water infrastructure

The team used the windtunneling process to examine each of the 10 strategy items in each scenario. The goal was a general assessment of how well the strategies would perform within and across the scenario set. Qualitative assessment with short descriptions, color coding, or symbols can be used to indicate the utility of the option in the context of the scenario (see figure 7.3).

In this case, the windtunneling process showed 4 core strategies out of the 10 that were ranked as "high utility" across all four scenarios:

- Develop targeted outreach to new [state] residents
- Explore and identify new revenue sources (taxes, royalties, fees)
- Offer "see and experience" wildlife tours
- Develop and provide resources for enhanced emergency management planning

The purpose of this exercise, once again, was to identify a small number of strategies that would become the foundation of action. The omitted six strategies are not off the table but may need more detailed study or may be scenario dependent. The results of this exercise give you a way to reduce the options to a manageable and actionable few and to understand which strategies will perform well across the different scenarios.

	Washington Monument Scenario	Central Park Scenario	Yosemite National Park Scenario	Denali National Park Scenario
Develop targeted outreach to new [state] residents	High utility	High utility	Medium utility	High utility
Explore and identify new revenue sources (taxes, royalties, fees)	High utility	High utility	High utility	High utility
Increase partnerships with public, private, and nongovernmental organizations	Low utility	Medium utility	Medium utility	Medium utility
Partner with education to enhance K–12 wildlife curriculum	Medium utility	High utility	Low utility	Medium utility
Offer "see and experience" wildlife tours	High utility	High utility	High utility	High utility
Restructure Fish and Wildlife Agency to regional offices	Low utility	Low utility	Low utility	Low utility
Develop and provide resources for enhanced emergency management planning	High utility	High utility	High utility	High utility
Engage partners and facilitate discussions on at-risk ecosystems	Medium utility	High utility	Medium utility	Medium utility
Invest in climate change analysis tools and programs	High utility	Low utility	Medium utility	Medium utility
Modify water infrastructure	Low utility	High utility	Low utility	Low utility

Figure 7.3. Windtunneling Generic Strategies for Fish and Wildlife Agency

Workshop Format and Guidelines: Windtunneling Generic Strategies

Time: 2–4 hours.
Participants: 5–15.

Assumptions: You have a set of scenarios and a set of generic strategies.

Workshop Format: Assemble the decision-making team in a live, online, or other meeting location and use the instructions below.

Instructions:

- Review scenario 1 to get into the mind-set of the dynamics it contains.
- Participants individually consider the set of strategies in scenario 1 in terms of how each strategy item will generally perform.
- Continue debate and dialogue until a general agreement is reached.
- Repeat the process for the remaining scenarios.

Products:

- A manageable set of core strategies that perform well across the set of scenarios

Adjusting Windtunneled Strategies for a Strategic Plan

As we saw in chapter 2, it is common for strategic plans to be vague and nonactionable. The items in a strategic plan have to be precise, and they have to include attention to the scope, schedule, and budget required. They must also include measurement criteria. While there are different views on what makes for the most useful strategic plan, a simple approach that accomplishes what is needed looks like this:

STRATEGY ITEM:
SCOPE:
SCHEDULE:
BUDGET:

- Develop targeted outreach to new [state] residents
- Explore and identify new revenue sources (taxes, royalties, fees)
- Offer "see and experience" wildlife tours
- Develop and provide resources for enhanced emergency management planning

To increase utility, these generic strategies need to be specified in terms of their scope, schedule, and budget. Using the four windtunneled generic strategies from Fish and Wildlife Agency as an example, the outcome looks like this:

STRATEGY ITEM 1: Develop targeted outreach to new [state] residents by creating customized lists of new residents and connecting to state resource databases. This will be a heavy resource draw on the marketing team.

SCOPE: Within six months, develop 10 connections or partnerships with state resources to track incoming new residents.

SCHEDULE: Within one year, have marketing send materials to all new state residents (new within the last 12 months).

BUDGET: Allocate 10 percent of the budget to support the marketing team in the development of new marketing materials, and allocate 5 percent of the budget to support developing contacts within the state system.

STRATEGY ITEM 2: Explore and identify new revenue sources (taxes, royalties, fees).

SCOPE: Within six months, identify five new potential revenue sources in the tax, royalties, and fees categories.

SCHEDULE: Within one year, secure at least two new funding sources accounting for at least 20 percent of current revenues.

BUDGET: Allocate 5 percent of the budget to support the identification of at least five new revenue sources.

STRATEGY ITEM 3: Offer "see and experience" wildlife tours.

SCOPE: Within six months, be able to offer five "see and experience" wildlife tours in which agency employees guide members of the public in unique wildlife experiences.

SCHEDULE: Within one year, offer these five experiences at least twice per quarter.

BUDGET: Allocate 10 percent of the budget to support the identification of at least five new revenue sources.

STRATEGY ITEM 4: Develop and provide resources for enhanced emergency management planning.

SCOPE: Within six months, double the availability of personal protective equipment for hospital workers and create a staffing plan for hospital use surges.

SCHEDULE: Within one year, have enough stock of personal protective equipment and staffing plans to accommodate a major disaster.

BUDGET: Allocate 10 percent of the budget to secure additional supplies required for disaster preparation.

Attaching scope, schedule, and budget requirements to strategy items immediately makes them more actionable.

Workshop Format and Guidelines: Adjusting Windtunneled Strategies for a Strategic Plan

Time: 2–4 hours.
Participants: 5–15.

Assumptions: You have outputs from chapter 6 (generic strategies, opportunities and threats, and/or adapt, mitigate, and thrive strategies).

Workshop Format: Assemble the scenario team and gather your strategies.

Instructions:

- Using the outputs from any of the exercises in chapter 6 (generic strategies, opportunities and threats, or adapt, mitigate, and thrive), consolidate and specify the list of common useful strategies across the scenarios.

- Finalize a manageable number of strategies (15 or fewer recommended).
- Windtunnel the strategies to find the most useful strategies across the set of scenarios.
- Clarify the scope, schedule, and budget for each item.

Summary

This chapter has explained how to use scenarios as wind tunnels to test strategies. The concept of windtunneling was described and examples were provided. The examples show you how to take your strategies through the set of scenarios in order to determine a set of strategies that work across all scenarios. The final part of this chapter showed how to make your final strategies more precise, measurable, and actionable. Using these processes and tools connects scenarios to strategies in important ways that are essential for advancing both fields.

8 ■ Testing Decisions and Options with Scenarios

Decision making is an important outcome of scenario planning (Schoemaker, 1993, 1995). While there is substantial research evidence, the advice on specific practices to guide decision making with scenario planning is lacking. One of the most powerful ways to use scenarios is for testing specific decisions. Scenarios are used as wind tunnels to understand the potential risks and benefits associated with possible options.

This more specific and useful way to use scenarios is based on having a defined decision with a set of options. For example, beginning with a decision to expand market share in California, related options could be to buy a firm, open an office, and strategically hire people in California with existing networks. These cases require a decision focus—scenarios are constructed with a decision in mind, though always with the external environment as the context (Chermack, 2004; Greiner et al., 2014; Wollenberg et al., 2000). Good scenarios should create insights that add to the list of options as new ideas are gained through studying multiple futures, but it does not always have to work that way. To get the most out of this approach, participants need to have the appropriate level of knowledge to assess the options. When they do, the outcome is an expert group analysis leading to preferred options within and across the scenarios.

This chapter describes how to use scenarios to test a decision and the related set of options. Because this is a more detailed and specific way to use scenarios, there are some requirements. First, the decision has to be defined: Acquire a firm? Expand into a new market? Reduce the product line? Second, the available options have to be clarified. These should be relatively detailed and action oriented. The main focus of the work is then to assess the potential risk and potential benefit of each option, in each scenario.

Generally, this approach uses yet another matrix. If risk is plotted on the vertical axis (the x axis) and benefit is plotted on the horizontal axis (the y axis), another matrix is apparent. Figure 8.1 shows the idea.

Building from this figure, it should be obvious that items falling into the "high benefit / low risk" category should be reserved for further examination. Likewise, items falling into the "low benefit / high risk" category should be considered as potential nonstrategies—strategy is also about what not to do. The "high benefit / high risk" items (upper right) are big-bet decisions. The concept is relatively

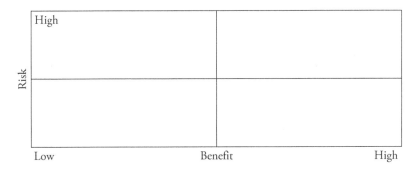

Figure 8.1. Generic Risk/Benefit Plotting

straightforward. This approach requires a specific focus from the start and is recommended when there is a clearly defined decision with associated options. It is best demonstrated with examples.

Example: Environmental Firm

An environmental firm (working mostly with municipalities on issues related to water and wastewater management) was looking to expand its presence and market share in California. The key focusing question for scenario building was, How could the California water/wastewater market evolve and change over the next five years? A series of workshops led to the development of four scenarios for the California water market. The resulting scenario matrix is in figure 8.2.

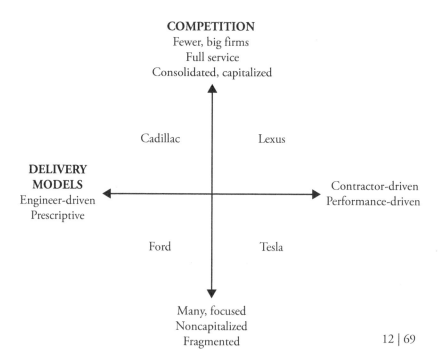

Figure 8.2. Environmental Firm's Scenario Matrix

Environmental Firm's Decision and Options

Once the scenarios were developed, the next step was to generate a set of potential options according to the decision focus. The decision focus was, How can we expand our California market share? Again, the intent was to expand market share in California, so the options were brainstormed. Of course, leaders already had particular options in mind, yet the goal was to generate a full list. After several meetings with team leaders, a final list of expansion options was determined:

1. Acquire regional firm
2. National partner in Los Angeles
3. Local partner in Los Angeles
4. Open office in Los Angeles
5. Open office in San Francisco
6. National partner in San Francisco
7. Local partner in San Francisco
8. Open office in Sacramento
9. Open office in San Jose
10. Integrated Project Delivery (IPD) partnerships
11. Client: California Water Service
12. Client: Great Oaks
13. Client: San Jose Water Co.
14. Client: Twin Valley
15. Client: Sierra City
16. Client: Lewis Small Water Co.

Once the options were identified (and several additional options came from reviewing the scenarios), the next step was to consider the potential outcome of each option in the context of each scenario. This is a more detailed version of the windtunneling activities described in the previous chapters.

A workshop was organized with a small team from Environmental Firm's leadership, and the goal was to evaluate the potential risk and benefit of each option in each scenario. Figure 8.3 shows the ranking sheet template that was distributed to each participant.

Option	Benefit	Risk
1. Acquire a regional firm Notes:		
2. National partner in Los Angeles Notes:		
3. Local partner in Los Angeles Notes:		
4. Open office in Los Angeles Notes:		
5. Open office in San Francisco Notes:		
6. National partner in San Francisco Notes:		
7. Local partner in San Francisco Notes:		
8. Open office in Sacramento Notes:		
9. Open office in San Jose Notes:		
10. IPD partnerships Notes:		
11. Target client: California Water Service Notes:		
12. Target client: Great Oaks Notes:		
13. Target client: San Jose Water Co. Notes:		
14. Target client: Twin Valley Notes:		
15. Target client: Sierra City Notes:		
16. Target client: Lewis Small Water Co. Notes:		

Figure 8.3. Potential Risk/Benefit Ranking Sheet

Participants were asked to read the Cadillac scenario and individually complete their own assessment of the potential risk and benefit for each option. Once participants completed their assessments, they discussed what they saw as the major areas of risk and benefit. Which options were the highest risk and why? Which options were the lowest risk and why? The conversation and debate allow for further dialogue, much like what happens in the scenario building process with the various sticky note ranking exercises.

Risk and Benefit Rankings of Environmental Firm's Options

Figures 8.4–8.8 show Environmental Firm's options ranked according to risk and benefit in each of the four scenarios that were developed.

You can see there are several good options under the dynamics of the Cadillac scenario (high benefit, low risk). Among these is attempting to win several specific clients (e.g., Lewis Small Water

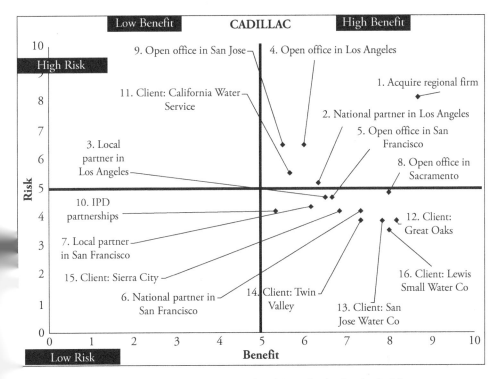

Figure 8.4. Environmental Firm's Potential Risk/Benefit Plot for the Cadillac Scenario

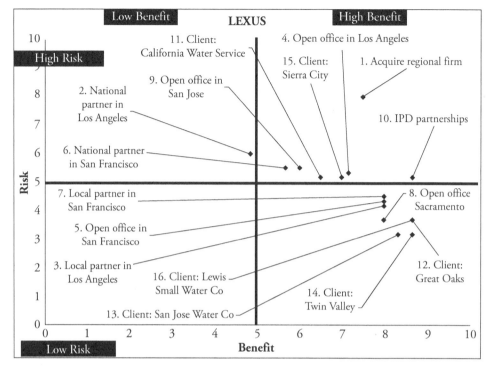

Figure 8.5. Environmental Firm's Potential Risk/Benefit Plot for the Lexus Scenario

Co., San Jose Water Co., and Great Oaks). There is also the option of opening an office in San Francisco. Again, the point is not to blindly follow the options that appear in the high benefit, low risk category; it is to identify what smaller set of options might be better under the Cadillac conditions.

Under the dynamics of the Lexus scenario, several of the same options appear to be useful (open an office in San Francisco; try to win contracts with Great Oaks, Twin Valley, and San Jose Water Co.). The plot has shifted somewhat, and the goal is to sift through the options, where they land on the plot, and consider which might require further research and analysis.

For the Tesla scenario, the options have shifted considerably. Far fewer really useful options are available in the Tesla scenario because it was a much more challenging scenario. Still, winning new clients seems to be the best of what is available.

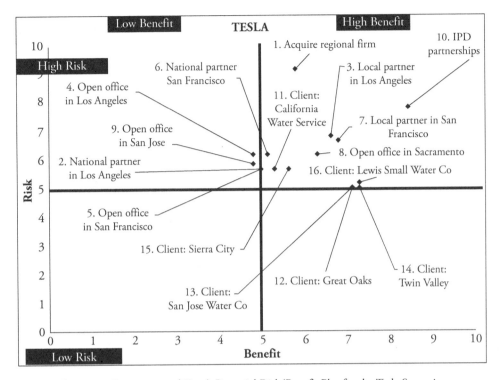

Figure 8.6. Environmental Firm's Potential Risk/Benefit Plot for the Tesla Scenario

For the conditions presented in the Ford F-150 scenario, there are again many helpful options; and again, they seem to converge around new clients. Overall, there is slightly more risk across the board in this scenario, yet the goal is the same: find the best options that might be studied more closely.

Finally, across the set of scenarios there are useful options that appear most resilient regardless of the scenario dynamics. Once again, new client work appears to be the best overall strategy for Environmental Firm. On review of these options, Environmental Firm executives identified the following options flagged for deeper study:

- New client: Lewis Small Water Co.
- New client: Great Oaks
- New client: Twin Valley
- New client: San Jose Water Co.

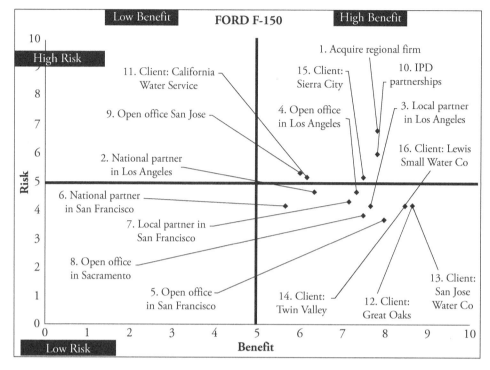

Figure 8.7. Environmental Firm's Potential Risk/Benefit Plot for the Ford F-150 Scenario

After reviewing the results, the executive team decided that the best overall strategy for expanding market share in California was to base it on developing new clients. As a result of this exercise (and the preparation that went into it), several clients were identified, which gave the executive team a place to start. The next steps were to understand which consultants in the organization might have contacts in the target client companies.

Workshop Outcomes

The potential risk/benefit ranking exercise focuses on the lower-right quadrant of the space. Items ranked "high benefit / low risk" are the target. It is not always easy to interpret the five plots that are generated through this activity, and thoughtfulness is important. It is not suggested that anything appearing in the lower-right quadrant simply be blindly followed, yet these options warrant further inves-

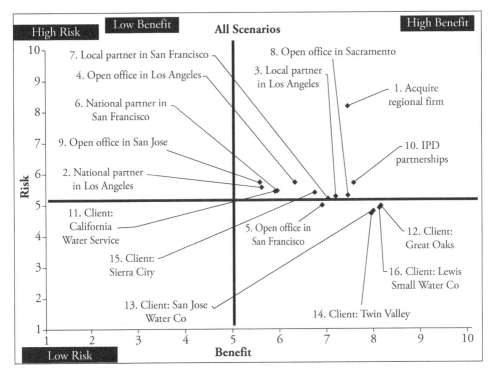

Figure 8.8. Environmental Firm's Potential Risk/Benefit Plot—All Scenarios

tigation. The assumption underlying this approach is that the participants involved in the ranking have deep insight into the context and decision being considered. If that is the case, you will come away with a group of experts thinking on the decision and relevant options being considered. At the conclusion of this exercise, options were identified for deeper analysis. In addition, some options were removed as they consistently appeared in the "high risk / low benefit" category.

Example: Oil & Gas Company

The Geology and Exploration Division of Oil & Gas Company, which has operations in Venezuela, discovered new reserves in the ground. The key question was, How do we finance the extraction of these resources? Scenarios were developed based on the sociopolitical

Figure 8.9. Scenario Matrix for Oil & Gas Company

context of the country, access to land, disruption of remote towns, and extraction logistics, among other uncertainties.

Using the 2 × 2 matrix approach, four scenarios were constructed (figure 8.9). These scenarios were framed on the valuation of resources in the ground and the sociopolitical environment. Once the scenarios were complete, attention turned toward a key decision.

Based on the scenario matrix, the four written scenarios were developed through intensive additional research, earlier participant interviews, and insights gained from the various workshops. Further work with the leadership team yielded a focused decision and options. Framed around the key decision of how to finance the massive project of extracting these new resources, several possible financing options were generated (figure 8.10).

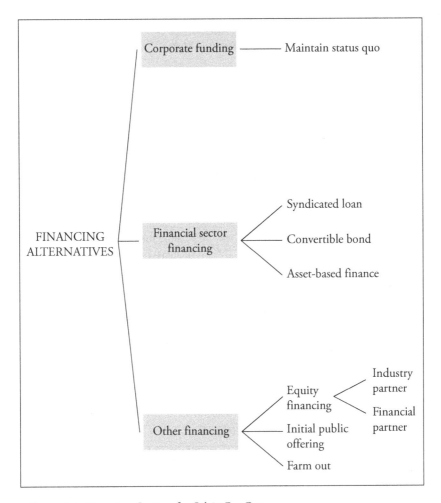

Figure 8.10. Financing Options for Oil & Gas Company

Several options emerged from the scenario exercise as insights were gained. For example, the idea of an initial public offering (IPO) came directly from workshop conversations on reviewing the scenarios. The next step was to design a workshop to consider each financing option in each scenario and to determine a set of optimal options that "worked" across the whole set of scenarios. Participants were asked to review the Mule scenario and complete a worksheet listing the financing options with potential risk and potential benefit rankings for each option. The ranking scale

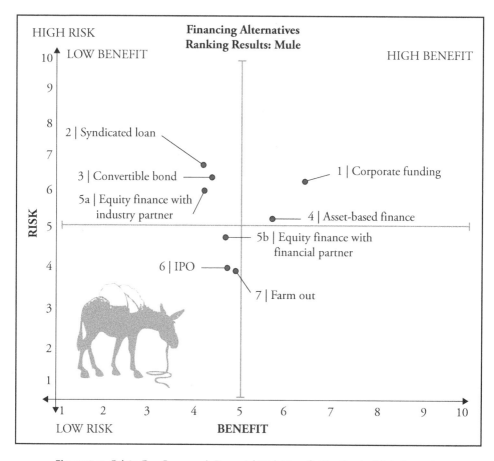

Figure 8.11. Oil & Gas Company's Potential Risk/Benefit Plot for the Mule Scenario

was 1–10 for both potential risk and potential benefit. To be clear, this was not a prioritizing activity: a ranking of 10 on risk could be used numerous times, and it was entirely acceptable for a given option to receive a ranking of 10 on both potential risk and potential benefit.

Participants completed the activity individually (in real time), and afterward a group conversation and reflection was facilitated. Participants engaged in dialogue around what they saw as particularly high risk / high benefit, what stood out, and what did not. After

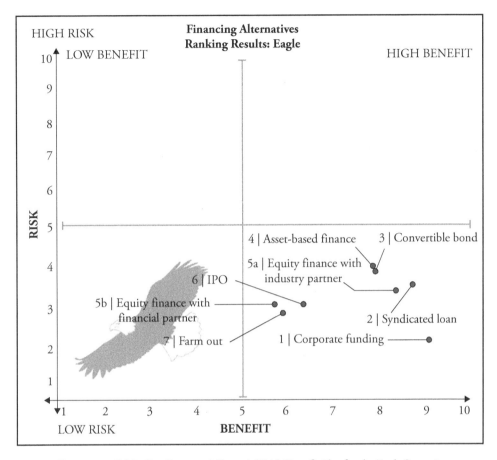

Figure 8.12. Oil & Gas Company's Potential Risk/Benefit Plot for the Eagle Scenario

30 minutes of group conversation, participants could change and finalize their rankings based on any insights or points of view that may have shifted their perceptions during the conversation. The facilitator collected their ranking worksheets, and the process was repeated for the Eagle, Salmon, and Porcupine scenarios. Once the workshop was complete, data were compiled and plotted on a potential risk/benefit matrix. Figures 8.11–8.15 show the outputs.

In the slightly difficult Mule scenario, there are few viable options. Seeking corporate funding has the highest potential benefit, but it

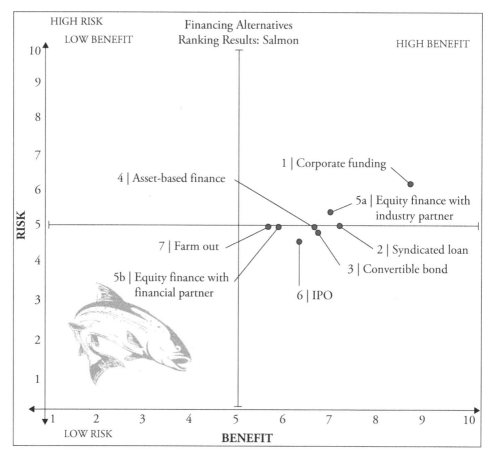

Figure 8.13. Oil & Gas Company's Potential Risk/Benefit Plot for the Salmon Scenario

also carries a bit of risk. Lower-risk options include farm out, IPO, and equity finance with a financial partner, but they are also lower in potential benefit.

In the more optimistic Eagle scenario, all options fell in the high benefit, low risk category. In this scenario, the environment favors Oil & Gas Company, and all options could be on the table.

The Salmon scenario provided some challenges that put the options toward the middle. Again, all options carry some risk under the circumstances. Of the set, a syndicated loan, convertible bond,

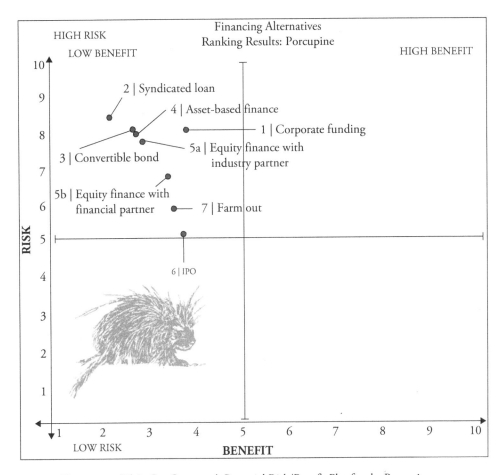

Figure 8.14. Oil & Gas Company's Potential Risk/Benefit Plot for the Porcupine Scenario

IPO, and equity financing with an industry partner are worth considering.

The most difficult scenario—the Porcupine scenario—did not leave much room for assessing viable options. In these conditions, the recommendation was to delay operations or abandon the project. An IPO could be an option to keep the project alive, but the risk outweighs the benefit.

Finally, across the set of scenarios, corporate funding, asset-based financing, and IPO carry possible value. In this situation,

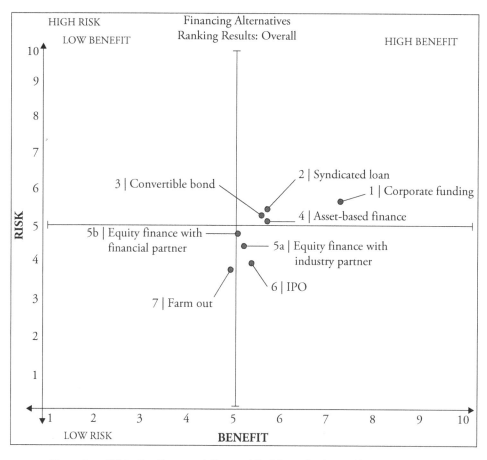

Figure 8.15. Oil & Gas Company's Potential Risk/Benefit Plot—All Scenarios

these options were recommended for more detailed study and analysis.

Of course, there can be problems with averaging averages, but these are not statistical exercises—they are practical exercises. The idea of combining ratings across people and across groups requires caution. It is never recommended that the resulting outputs are simply followed blindly. It is important to recognize that the outcomes are based on participant perceptions of potential risk and benefit, which is why it is so critical that the participants really understand the issue, decision, and options. The purpose of this workshop is to vet the options down to a manageable few that can be studied more closely and potentially implemented.

Granularity and Comparability of Options

One important lesson in working with decisions and options is to ensure there is granularity and comparability of the options. To clarify, in order for the assessment of potential risk and benefit to be useful, the options need to be at least roughly similar. For example, in the Environmental Firm example above, there was a real lack of comparability. Acquiring a firm in California is far more resource intensive than making a few strategic hires in California. In this case, the assessment of potential risk and benefit was difficult because the options were so varied.

To correct for this, once a list of options is generated, it is extremely useful to consider a general scope, schedule, and budget for each option before working through potential risk and benefit rankings. Once this is accomplished, the options can be grouped into similar categories and the assessment of potential risk and benefit can be completed for each category of similar options. This will make the assessment of potential risk and benefit more accurate and useful. In the Oil & Gas Company example above, there was considerable alignment among the options: there were eight different financing options to retrieve the newly discovered resources from the ground.

Workshop Format and Guidelines: Decisions and Options

Time: 4 hours.
Participants: 5–15.

Assumptions: You have a set of scenarios and a defined decision with a set of options.

Workshop Format: The purpose of this workshop is to assess the potential risk and potential benefit of specific options in each scenario and across the set of scenarios. This is an activity that requires individual input as well as group dialogue and debate.

Instructions:

- Participants read scenario 1 and individually consider the potential risk and potential benefit of each option in scenario 1.
- Participants write their rankings (1–10) on the worksheet.
- Participants discuss their individual rankings and identify options of high risk and benefit overall (consensus is not required).
- Repeat this process for each scenario.
- When the process is complete for all scenarios, input rankings into an Excel file (or other software) to generate risk/benefit plots.
- Using the Excel tool, filter by scenario to display the potential risk and potential benefit plots.
- Find the options that collect in the "high benefit / low risk" quadrant as viable options.
- Find the options that collect in the "high risk / low benefit" quadrant as options that might be removed.

Summary

This chapter has demonstrated how to use a set of scenarios to understand the potential risks and benefits of specific options for a decision. Using scenarios in this way is a more specific version of windtunneling, and the goal is to find options that are beneficial in multiple or all scenarios. Another goal is to identify options that don't make sense under any circumstances and can therefore be removed from the list of possible options or actions. This approach is extremely useful in reducing the list of possible options down to a manageable few that can be studied further and potentially implemented.

9 ■ Assessing the Financial Benefits of Scenarios

Assessing the financial benefits of organizational interventions is increasingly important work (Long et al., 2020). With continued pressure on financial resources, decision makers have to justify investments and demonstrate that they will be worthwhile (Baah et al., 2020; Nickell & Nicolitsas, 1999). To convince leaders that the investment is worth the outcome requires evidence. Historically, those working in change management, training, leadership, strategy, and other related domains do not have strong track records of demonstrating the financial benefits of their programs. All of these activities can be viewed as interventions in organizations, and it is critical to think about the value they can provide.

Scenario planning is a process that operates within an organization and its context (Ramirez & Wilkinson, 2016). The purpose of scenario planning revolves around understanding the external environment, how it could change, and making uncertainty part of the planning process. There is no question that scenario planning involves specific organizational titles, departments, functions, workshops, participant selection, program design, and facilitation. These subcomponents of scenario planning all have costs in terms of time, effort, and financial investment. When scenarios are used to guide decision making, there should be an expectation that those decisions will have outcomes. Decision outcomes can almost always be connected to financial value. Yet, this perspective on scenario planning has not yet appeared in the available guidance. Why?

One answer further highlights the need for this book: scenarios are not often applied and used. In the rare cases that they are used, the process does not reach far enough to get to financial outcomes that can be attributed to the scenario work. It is important to change this practice.

Because there are no publicly available examples of how to estimate the return on investment or specific financial gains from scenario planning, this chapter borrows from other realms of organizational activity that have successfully made the link. However, examples are provided from my own work over the past several years that has integrated the concepts with practice. In particular, Swanson's (2001) overall framework for assessing the financial benefits of human resource development is adjusted, adopted, and applied to the process of scenario planning. The next section describes the basic principles for assessing the financial benefits of any program. After these principles are presented, the more specific critical outcome technique (COT) is reviewed as the best way to assess the financial benefits of scenario planning because of its post hoc nature. Finally, three examples of applying the COT to scenario planning projects are provided. The purpose of this chapter is to show you how to assess the financial benefits of scenario planning.

Basic Principles for Assessing Financial Benefits

There are four foundational principles for assessing the financial benefits of any organizational activity: (1) the benefit assessment model, (2) the forecasting financial benefit model, (3) the actual financial benefit model, and (4) the approximated financial benefit model

(Swanson, 2001). These principles are reviewed before a specific approach for use with scenario planning is presented.

Benefit Assessment Model

The basic benefit assessment model includes *performance value, cost,* and *benefit* as its components. These components are arranged in a simple and elegant equation:

Performance value	(Performance value resulting from the program or intervention)
−Cost	(Cost of the program or intervention)
Benefit	(Benefit is the performance value minus the cost)

Using this equation requires specifying the values of each. Obviously, you only need to understand the performance value and the cost to get to the benefit. Underneath this foundational model are three different approaches to thinking about benefits that have implications for determining the performance value. Again, they are the forecasting model, the actual model, and the approximated model.

Forecasting Financial Benefit Model

Forecasting the financial benefit means suggesting a benefit from the start. By definition, this is an expected benefit, and reality may not follow along with expectations. Still, the forecasting benefit method is useful for suggesting to decision makers that the program will result in positive financial outcomes. This is the "before the fact" method—before implementation (Swanson, 2001, p. 32). When thinking about using the forecasting benefit method related to scenario planning, it is helpful to have some details about the purpose of the project. For example, if leaders are thinking about investing in scenario planning to test a decision about acquiring a firm, the forecasting method would estimate the potential benefits of acquiring the firm, with certain assumptions to support the estimates. However, it may not be the best approach for thinking about the financial benefits of scenario planning.

Actual Financial Benefit Model

The actual financial benefit method is used "in process"—during the program or intervention. With this method, the assessment is ongoing throughout the work and tracks the assessment data as the intervention unfolds. Specific and planned costs and benefits are recorded. This method doesn't really get at outcomes that could take weeks or months to emerge, and therefore it is not recommended for use with scenario planning.

Approximated Financial Benefit Model

The approximated method of assessing financial benefits focuses on "after the fact" analysis. It is most useful when decisions or actions that resulted from a program have shown a benefit. For this reason, it is the best method for assessing the financial benefits of scenario planning. Within this method, there are specific techniques, and the COT is most appropriate for use with scenarios and strategy. It is important to note that the approximated method has important implications for determining the performance value. Because this method is applied after the fact, it means the performance value is based on a *desired* performance outcome. Performance outcomes can be clarified by applying the more specific COT within the approximated method.

The COT

Because the decisions made or actions taken as a result of scenario planning take time to show effects, the COT is recommended. It falls in the category of approximated financial benefit. "The Critical Outcome Technique (COT) is a practical evaluation system that can be applied to many performance improvement programs" (Mattson, 2005, p. 102). The COT was developed in response to demands for financial valuation of seemingly "soft" organizational efforts and managers' preferences for clear business results (see figure 9.1). It is simple, elegant, and focused on post hoc assessment. This requires time to observe and assess the results of any intervention or program. The COT focuses on *critical* outcomes, which can be defined as "(a) business results at the organizational, process, or individual levels,

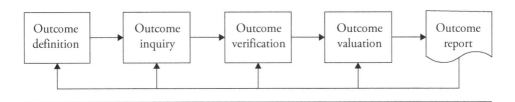

Figure 9.1. Model of the Critical Outcome Technique (COT)

and / or (b) financial results or benefits in monetary terms" (Mattson, 2005, p. 103), and proceeds through the following phases:

1. Determine (post hoc) the intended outcomes of the program.
2. Collect data from program concerning the attainment of the outcomes.
3. Validate this information through a source other than the participant (e.g., the participant's supervisor or manager).
4. Determine the performance value for each of the outcomes.
5. Produce a summary report of the evaluation findings for key stakeholders.

When scenario planning is viewed as an organizational intervention (just like leadership development, training, and change management, among others), the COT is the most appropriate way to think about how to assess the financial results. The COT has five key phases: (1) outcome definition, (2) outcome inquiry, (3) outcome verification, (4) outcome valuation, and (5) the outcome report. Each of these is briefly described, followed by examples of the COT being applied to scenario planning.

Outcome Definition

The first phase in the COT is outcome definition. The point is to consider the level of performance that will be affected. In organizations, these are commonly the individual, team, process, and organizational levels. Individual-level outcomes include knowledge, skills, and abilities. Team-level outcomes commonly and obviously include team performance. Process-level outcomes usually involve improving or redesigning processes for efficiency gains. Finally, organizational-level performance refers to outcomes at the enterprise level. The related component of outcomes that needs to be considered is outcome drivers. Outcome drivers are the factors that can be changed in order to have an impact on performance. "Taken together, performance outcomes and drivers illustrate the potential cause and effect relationship between a program and performance at a given level" (Mattson, 2005, p. 104). In the context of scenario planning, the level of performance will almost always be the organizational level. Outcome drivers will usually be the strategic decisions or actions that could be taken, which ultimately result in an expected benefit.

Defining the timing of when to assess outcomes also occurs in this phase. It is dependent on the intervention or program. This is why the COT is usually applied in the weeks or months following any intervention or program. The post hoc nature of the method requires a period of time in which to understand if the target outcomes have been affected. With scenarios, an appropriate time frame is four to six months, but it can be longer. These time frames should allow for the effects of scenarios on decisions and actions to be apparent. Depending on the desired outcomes, assessments can be made as to the benefits of the scenario exercises.

Outcome Inquiry

Outcome inquiry is simply the process of identifying the appropriate data about the program via surveys, interviews, reports, or other forms of data. Aiming for objective data is important; relying solely on perception data is a misstep. Investment decisions and reallocation of resources could be common objective data sources. Assuming that decisions and actions have been made as a result of scenario planning, there should be obvious measures of the success or failure of those decisions or actions.

Outcome Verification

Outcome verification involves multiple participants in the assessment of program effectiveness. Anyone responsible for a program will likely

Company	
Program:	
Date:	
Participants:	
Program Purpose and Description:	
Evaluation Summary:	
Business Results:	Financial Results:
Approval:	
Distribution List:	

Figure 9.2. Outcome Report Template

argue in its favor, and the purpose of involving several participants in this phase is to reduce bias and gain multiple perspectives.

Outcome Valuation

Outcome valuation is the actual process of collecting the data specified in the previous phases and attaching a financial value to the outcomes. Outcome valuation can be based on financial models, the actual dollar value of a significant investment made, or the estimated return on investment.

Outcome Report

The final step is to produce an outcome report. This simple report shows the details related to the program, clarifies the parts of the program, and summarizes the effectiveness of the program (see figure 9.2).

Examples

Following are two examples of applying the COT to scenario planning projects. In the first, a simple example with Propane Company, the focal decision is whether to acquire a firm. This example shows how the COT can be used to assess the financial benefits of an expensive investment with a high degree of risk. In the second example, Oil & Gas Company uses the COT to understand how its financing decisions performed six months after the scenario project was completed. It is a retrospective example that compares the option it chose with all the others. With the tools in this chapter and the examples provided for guidance, you should be able to assess the financial benefit of any scenario planning exercise, given sufficient time for the outcomes to show.

Example: Propane Company

In 2016, Propane Company was looking for options to expand its market share. Part of the potential strategy was to acquire a smaller independent provider, and several possible targets were being considered. Eventually, the financial analysts settled on an independent provider that seemed to be the most appealing investment option. Organization leaders decided to use scenario planning as a way to test the decision of acquiring the independent provider. Scenarios were created, and the team windtunneled the major decision in the scenarios. In the end, they decided to move ahead with the acquisition as the scenarios showed it to be a beneficial decision across the scenarios. Twelve months later, an assessment of the financial benefits was conducted using the COT.

> OUTCOME DEFINITION AND TIMING: Organizational level—timing is 12 months after scenario planning.
>
> OUTCOME INQUIRY: Potential increases to overall organizational revenue after 12 months expected to be $6 million based on retaining 87 percent of acquired customer base and winning an additional 10 percent of market share in the surrounding geographic area to the original independent provider's area.
>
> OUTCOME VERIFICATION: The entire leadership team (12 people) was involved in the assessment of acquiring the firm, using a set of four scenarios as their test, and all agreed that the outcome verification was reasonable.
>
> OUTCOME VALUATION: $6 million
>
> OUTCOME REPORT (SEE FIGURE 9.3):

Company: Propane Company	
Program: Scenario planning for firm acquisition	
Date: August 2017	
Participants: Leadership team, finance team, strategy team	
Program Purpose and Description: The goal of this scenario planning project was to develop scenarios for the future of the propane industry using a five-year timeline. Because of expansion opportunities, we specifically intended to use the scenarios to examine the possibility of acquiring a target firm.	
Evaluation Summary: As a result of assessing the risks and benefits of acquiring a firm across a set of four scenarios, it was decided to proceed with acquiring the target firm. The perspective of the leadership is that the scenarios allowed us to see multiple positive circumstances under which acquiring the target firm would likely increase organizational revenues. Twelve months after the scenario project was concluded, and at the time of this report, the target firm has contributed $15 million to overall organizational revenues.	
Business Results: – Decision to proceed with acquiring a firm – 10% increase in new customers – 87% of existing clients retained with new contracts having improved margin – Total financial effect	**Financial Results:** –$6 million –$9 million $15 million
Approval: [CEO]	
Distribution List: Leadership team and board of directors	

Figure 9.3. Propane Company Outcome Report

Once these figures were determined, the team could apply the benefit assessment model as follows:

$15 million	(Performance value of decisions made owing to the scenario project)
−$200,000	(Cost of the scenario planning project, including participant time)
$14.8 million	(Benefit)

In this case, the timeline for outcome assessment was longer than usual, but it was appropriate for the decision and how long it would take to see an impact. The outcome valuation also exceeded the expectations. This example shows that there are times when scenarios can help guide highly significant decisions, and the benefits can far exceed the costs.

Example: Oil & Gas Company

The case of Oil & Gas Company demonstrates the application of the COT method for assessing the financial benefits of scenario planning. If you recall from chapter 8, Oil & Gas Company identified several resources in the ground in Venezuela. Scenarios were built around the context, social dynamics, and technical dynamics related to how to extract the resources. Oil & Gas Company leaders considered seven different options for financing the massive project:

1. Corporate funding
2. Syndicated loan
3. Convertible bond
4. Asset-based finance
5. Equity finance with industry partner
6. Equity finance with financial partner
7. IPO

The team windtunneled the seven financing options through the scenarios and determined that seeking corporate financing was the most resilient strategy. It was also the lowest-cost option in the long run.

Company: Oil & Gas Company

Program: Scenario planning for resource extraction in Venezuela
Date: October 2018
Participants: Leadership team, finance team, strategy team
Program Purpose and Description: The goal of this scenario planning project was to create different scenarios for the future of Oil & Gas Company's operations in Venezuela and to determine an optimal financing strategy for extracting resources. We used the scenarios to test different financing options given the costs associated with the major project of resource extraction. The scenarios clearly showed that the most resilient financing strategy was corporate funding. All other options had, at minimum, higher costs across the scenarios, and most included significant risk of assets or reduced profit due to partnerships.
Evaluation Summary: Six months after proceeding with corporate financing, we compared the financial position we chose with all other options.

Business Options:	Costs:
1. Corporate funding 2. Syndicated loan 3. Convertible bond 4. Asset-based finance 5. Equity finance with industry partner 6. Equity finance with financial partner 7. IPO	1. $25 billion over 10 years = $25 billion 2. Base + 7.2% interest over 10 years 3. Base + 8.1% interest over 10 years 4. Base + 10% interest over and risk of currently held assets 5. Base + 10% interest over and risk of currently held assets 6. Base + 10% interest and risk of currently held assets 7. Base + devaluation of company stock and assets
Total financial effect of the decision to use corporate funding (directly attributable to the scenario project)	The range of savings due to corporate financing is between $1.8 billion and $5.5 billion, with no assets or profits at risk.

Approval: [CEO]
Distribution List: Leadership team and board of directors

Figure 9.4. Oil & Gas Company Outcome Report

OUTCOME DEFINITION AND TIMING: Organizational level—
  timing is six months after scenario planning.
OUTCOME INQUIRY: The most resilient option of the seven
  was judged to be corporate financing, and so that was the
  option selected. This was because there were no additional
  costs associated with "borrowing" the funding. All other
  options carried a cost.
OUTCOME VERIFICATION: The entire leadership team (19
  people) was involved in the assessment of the available
  financing options, using a set of four scenarios as their test,
  and all agreed that the outcome verification was reasonable.
OUTCOME VALUATION: The cost to finance the entire extraction process over approximately 10 years was $25 billion.
  The financing options are compared in the outcome report.
OUTCOME REPORT: (see figure 9.4)

Once again, using scenarios to examine critically strategic decisions led to a significant benefit. In this case the benefits were in savings on interest, maintaining profits by avoiding partnerships and
keeping all assets protected. This example uses the cost savings to
derive the benefit, and these figures can still be used in the benefit
assessment model.

$1.8–$5.5 billion	(Performance value of decisions made owing to the scenario project)
−$200,000	(Cost of the scenario planning project— including participant time)
$1.6–$5.3 billion	(Benefit)

Summary

Assessing the outcomes and financial benefits of scenario planning
is the surest way to demonstrate the value it can offer. This activity
is critical to advancing scenarios. This chapter has introduced the
basic principles for assessing the financial benefits of organizational
programs. Further, it has specifically reviewed the COT because of

how well it lends itself to assessing scenario planning outcomes. Two examples of using the COT to assess scenario financial benefits have been presented along with the structure and templates that allow you to apply it. While the figures they present may seem outrageous, using scenarios to inform significant investment decisions can return these kinds of benefits. The point is that a single, big decision can have financial effects in the millions or billions of dollars (positive or negative). The key is to track the decision making back to the scenario effort. Financial assessment of scenario planning doesn't have to be overly complicated or take a long time. Using the tools presented in this chapter can be relatively simple if the COT outcome categories are defined and applied. Using them effectively will require patience and persistence. Ultimately, assessing the financial benefits of scenario planning means holding scenario planners accountable for using their scenarios and following through to show their value. This activity takes one more step in linking scenarios to strategy for improving organizations.

10 ■ Modeling Financials with Scenarios

Financial analysts often rule the organizations in which they live (Smith et al., 2011). Their analyses tend to capture the attention of leadership in two important categories: (1) quarterly earnings and (2) return to shareholders (Gelles & Yaffe-Bellany, 2019). In most cases the board's expectations are a direct result of the model built by the finance team. The reality is that most companies and CEOs are held to their boards' expectations. The demand for a quarterly financial growth outcome is hardly supportive of organizational longevity (Collingwood, 2001; Millon, 2002; Zhang & Gimeno, 2016). Squeezing as much profit as possible out of any organization—regardless of the impact on people, expertise, workforce capacity, communities, states, and nations—has become the norm (Guerrera, 2009). Indeed, the focus on short-term gains has almost replaced the idea of a long-lived organization.

Once again, it is probably unfair to start this chapter so harshly, though the reality is difficult to deny. The purpose is not to unfairly rake the finance officers over the coals, yet it is hard to ignore the influence and the tremendous impact on strategy given that over 90 percent of Fortune 100 companies put strategy in their finance departments (Benninga, 2014; Gelsomino et al., 2019; Kono & Barnes, 2010). To be fair, no activity within an organization should be supported if there is not an expectation of something gained (Swanson, 2001; Swanson et al., 1999.). Investments in activities like scenario planning, leadership development, and training should be expected to produce something of value. Without that, there is no reason to proceed.

Scenario planners have long avoided the need to demonstrate the financial results of their projects. Imagining futures can be a fun and creative activity—and it can lead to insights. But unless those insights can connect to doing something differently that can have a measurable impact, there is a risk that scenarios will be dismissed as something interesting but without real value.

There is no advice for connecting scenario planning activity to forecasted organizational performance. Many will say it is too difficult and that there are too many other variables that could influence financial performance. Yes, these arguments are partially true. It is not easy to estimate the potential impact of scenario planning on organizational financial performance, and many variables play a part in organizational performance into the future. However, just because something is difficult does not mean we shouldn't pay attention to it. With some adjustment, it is possible to *estimate* the ways in which scenarios could affect an organizational financial model, and it is possible to *estimate* the effects of scenarios on firm performance.

Scenario planning has to be linked to financial outcomes in order for it to be accepted as a common organizational practice. Because scenarios deal with the future (just like financial models), it is not necessary to have finite and actual financial outcomes. We cannot predict the future. But it is possible to estimate the impacts of scenarios and the events they contain on the current financial modeling. This requires bringing the finance people into scenarios and attempting to spark their creativity. While this may seem a difficult task (finance people are not often known for their creativity), there is one important thing that scenarios and financial models have in common: assumptions.

The purpose of this chapter is to describe specific ways that scenarios can be connected to financial models. This chapter will cover the following:

- What a financial model is
- How financial models are used
- How to connect scenarios and financial models

What Is a Financial Model?

A financial model is an estimate of a business's forecast of earnings into the future (Benninga, 2014). Usually, it is based on a set of assumptions for how the business will perform. Aligned with strategic planning (and the assumption that the world will not change), most companies work on a single financial model. Most financial models are built on the organization's historical performance and then projections are made into the future.

Different Types of Financial Models

There are five types of financial models: (1) the three-statement model, (2) discounted cash flow analysis model, (3) leveraged-buyout model, (4) merger and acquisition model, and (5) sensitivity analysis (Pignataro, 2013). By far, the most common of these is the three-statement model. The others are used for more specific purposes. The three-statement financial model consists of the income statement, balance sheet, and cash flow statement. Of these, the balance sheet is the most important. Figure 10.1 provides a generic balance sheet.

How Financial Models Are Used

Financial models are generally used to estimate expected organizational performance into the future. They are used to make decisions about how to raise capital and grow the business and are also

	2018	2019	2020	2021	2022	2023
Assets						
Cash						
Accounts receivable						
Inventory						
Current assets						
Property & equipment						
Goodwill						
Total assets						
Liabilities						
Short-term debt						
Accounts payable						
Current liabilities						
Long-term debt						
Total liabilities						
Shareholder's equity						
Equity capital						
Retained earnings						
Shareholder's equity						
Total liabilities & shareholder's equity						
Net Profit						

Figure 10.1. Generic Balance Sheet

used in planning, accounting, allocating capital, and potential merger and acquisition activity. Financial models are used to understand the value of the business and include the major levers for making decisions (e.g., income, assets, debt).

Using Financial Models with Scenarios

Bringing scenarios and financial models together creates an opportunity to explore multiple financial models—one for each scenario. The goal of using financial models with scenarios is to consider forecasts of the most important aspects of organizational performance into the future and attach them to each scenario—in other words, to consider how the financial model might change according to the dynamics of each scenario. There is no right answer to the activities described in this chapter; they are speculative.

It is tempting to think that financial models are based on objective data. In fact, financial models require just as many assumptions as scenarios. Financial models are, by definition, estimates. Many of the principles in chapter 9 apply to using financial models within and across a set of scenarios. Instead of estimating the potential benefits or losses around specific actions or decisions, using financial models is intended to look at the organization as a whole.

Because scenarios and financial models make assumptions, there is a logical starting point for connecting the two. Common assumptions in financial models include industry growth, inflation, interest rates, currency rates, capital expenditures, market share, and taxes. Overlooking the fact that financial models make assumptions is one of the reasons they are so seductive and sometimes blindly adopted. The reality is that financial models are every bit as speculative as scenarios. Often, scenarios contain the same or very similar assumptions. Finding the overlap between the scenario assumptions and the financial model assumptions creates the ability to estimate the potential financial impact to the organization.

Most organizations use Workday Financials or Oracle Financials, and most finance teams download their financials to Microsoft Excel, play with them, and when satisfied, upload them back. The resulting model often becomes the decision-making frame used by the CEO and the board, as suggested above. The main problem with this approach is that managing entirely by the numbers usually doesn't turn out well (Foroohar, 2019). Even the classic management guru W. Edwards Deming (1991) included managing by the numbers as a cardinal sin. Looking at the numbers in a few different ways recognizes their instability and reveals options.

Putting scenarios together with financial models means breaking the dedication to a specific set of financial assumptions that often go unchecked. It means identifying those assumptions and making them clear. Once that is done, there is room to explore a few different versions of organizational performance based on what the scenarios have to offer.

Using Financial Models with Scenarios

There are two main ways to think about bringing scenarios and financial models together. The first is to estimate how the major indicators of organizational performance are potentially impacted by the dynamics of each scenario. The second is to consider the overall effects of scenario planning on the preferred financial model after they have been used for decision making. These two ways to connect scenarios and financial models are practical ways of assessing scenario impacts on organizational performance.

The balance sheet provided in figure 10.1 is overkill for the purpose of connecting scenarios and financial models. Figure 10.2 presents a simplified financial model adjusted for use with scenarios. This model includes the most important indicators of organizational performance that are likely to be affected by the dynamics that scenarios generally contain. Of course, financial models may have different parts depending on organizational accounting and finance preferences, but the main elements are there. This version will do

	Current Model	Scenario 1	Scenario 2	Scenario 3	Scenario 4
Revenues					
Core revenue sources					
Other					
Total revenues					
Cost of Sales					
Cost of core sales					
Other					
Gross Profit					
Operating Expenses					
Depreciation and amortization expense					
General and administrative expense					
Operating expense - lease expense					
Loss on asset sales and divestitures					
Operating Income					
Interest expense					
Loss on extinguishment of debt					
Other income					
Income tax expense (benefit)					
Net Profit					

Figure 10.2. Scenario Financial Model Template

the job, or you can create your own. The essential elements should be revenues, major costs, operating expenses, operating income, and, of course, net profit.

Example: Healthcare Organization

In a recent scenario project for Healthcare Organization, there was an opportunity to explore how the assumptions of scenarios could affect the financial model. While many of the activities described in this book were used, the final task was to interpret how the financial model could be impacted by the conditions of the scenarios. Once the finance team was able to review the scenarios, there were clear implications for expected revenues and costs of sales (figure 10.3).

Because of confidentiality, it is not appropriate to provide in full detail how the figures were estimated and the organizational context. But the idea should be easy to understand. For example, under scenario 1, the finance team saw that the conditions of the scenario would have a negative impact on organizational revenue sources. In addition, there was a perception that costs of sales would increase. You can see the impact to the net profit. Scenario 2 involved more favorable conditions, which led to an assumption of increased revenues. Cost of sales also increased owing to the expenses associated with expected organizational growth in that scenario. This activity provided a snapshot of how each scenario would impact organizational finances. Scenario 4 involved opportunities for growth that supported significant revenue increases. Of course, none of these options offered enough evidence to say with certainty which would come to be.

The important takeaway is that scenarios allow for exploring the expectations of revenues and costs that change according to different environmental conditions. Thinking through the implications for organizational performance overall is critical to getting away from a single financial model and the revenue projections that usually accompany it. In short, scenarios should be used to question the assumptions of the financial model, just as they are used to question assumptions for major decisions or investments.

	Current Model	Scenario 1	Scenario 2	Scenario 3	Scenario 4
Revenues					
Core revenue sources	$918,000	$735,800	$983,500	$893,000	$1,210,300
Other	$52,000	$43,000	$64,500	$52,000	$52,000
Total revenues	$970,000	$778,000	$1,048,000	$945,000	$1,262,300
Cost of Sales					
Cost of core sales	$315,000	$325,000	$357,000	$318,000	$368,000
Other	$18,000	$18,000	$18,000	$18,000	$18,000
Gross Profit	$636,200	$435,000	$673,000	$609,000	$876,300
Operating Expenses					
Depreciation and amortization expense	$110,000	$110,000	$110,000	$110,000	$110,000
General and administrative expense	$21,000	$21,000	$36,400	$18,800	$21,000
Operating expense - lease expense	$8,200	$8,200	$8,200	$8,200	$8,200
Loss on asset sales and divestitures	$8,200	$8,200	$8,200	$15,800	$8,200
Operating Income	$486,500	$287,600	$510,200	$456,200	$728,900
Interest expense	$3,000	$3,000	$3,000	$3,000	$3,000
Loss on extinguishment of debt	$				
Other income	$				
Income tax expense (benefit)	$100	$100	$100	$100	$100
Net Profit	$483,400	$283,900	$507,100	$453,100	$725,000

Figure 10.3. Modeling Healthcare Organization's Financials with Scenarios

Workshop Format and Guidelines: Modeling Scenario Financials

Time: 2 hours.
Participants: 5.

Assumptions: You have a set of scenarios and an existing financial model.

Workshop Format: This activity can be done in a workshop format, or by providing the scenarios to the finance team along with the instructions below.

Instructions:

- Assemble the finance team.
- Ask participants to read scenario 1 and consider the implications for organizational performance.
- Adjust the major categories on the scenario financial model and fill in the columns for each scenario.
- Repeat this process for the remaining scenarios.

Overall Financial Model across a Set of Scenarios

Another opportunity to think about connecting scenarios and financial models happens after the scenarios have been used and decisions have been made. The goal is to estimate how the scenario exercise overall may have impacted the critical elements of the financial model. Staying with the Healthcare Organization example, figure 10.4 provides an estimate of the overall scenario exercise on expected organizational finances. In this case, decisions were made as a result of the scenarios that led to increased revenue from new customers, higher prices, and other new revenue sources. To be more specific, the scenario work was with the IT department of Healthcare Organization, and the scenarios contained situations that would require a work-from-home option. While the scenarios did not contain a pandemic, they did contain other events that forced offices to close and people to work remotely (with the support of IT). Healthcare Organization was able to support a work-from-home option within

			Overall Scenario Planning Impact
Revenues			
	Core revenue sources	$ 918,000.00	Increased revenue owing to new customers, increased sales at current customers, higher prices on current products and services
	Other	$ 52,000.00	New sources of revenue directly attributable to scenario-related initiatives
	Total revenues	$ 970,000.00	
Cost of Sales			
	Cost of core sales	$ 315,800	Automation, efficiency, process improvement, raw material savings, contract efficiency
	Other	$ 18,000	New cost of sales directly attributable to scenario-related initiatives
Gross Profit		$ 636,200	
Operating Expenses		$ 110,800	
Depreciation and amortization expense		$ 21,000	Asset utilization
General and administrative expense		$ 8,200	Corporate back-office entities would be accounted for here
Operating expense - lease expense		$ 8,200	Asset lease expense
Loss on asset sales and divestitures		$ 1,500	
Operating Income		$ 486,500	
Interest expense		$ 3,000	Interest expense on debt
Loss on extinguishment of debt		$ -	
Other income		$ -	
Income tax expense (benefit)		$ 100	Tax
Net Profit		$ 483,400	

Figure 10.4. Overall Scenario Financial Model for Healthcare Organization

48 hours of the state's critical stay-at-home order due to the COVID-19 pandemic. Sometimes, scenarios do not get the exact events right, but the implications are almost identical.

Workshop Format and Guidelines: Overall Scenario Financial Models

Time: 2 hours.
Participants: 5.

Assumptions: You have a set of scenarios, four to six months have passed since you developed your scenarios, decisions and/or allocations have been made, and you have an existing financial model.

Workshop Format: This activity can be done in a workshop format, or by providing the scenarios to the finance team along with the instructions below.

Instructions:

- Assemble the finance team.
- Ask participants to read scenario 1 and consider the implications for organizational performance, given recent decision making and/or resource allocation.
- Adjust the major categories on the scenario financial model and fill in the columns for each scenario.
- Repeat this process for the remaining scenarios.

Summary

CEOs, finance officers, and managers of complex organizations have options when thinking about how scenarios can be useful. It is well documented that scenarios can help people think differently (Brooks & Curnin, 2021; Chermack, 2004) and expand their views of how the environment could change in surprising ways (Rickards et al., 2014). To get the most out of scenario planning requires commitment and discipline in using scenarios to understand the many ways that environmental changes can challenge the organization and its financial security. To do this effectively means paying attention to the outcomes of scenario planning at multiple levels of the organization, including its overall financial health. This can be difficult work that requires financial estimation and assumptions.

This chapter has described how scenarios can be used to challenge the overall organizational financial model and examine it in a few different ways. Scenarios are not just conceptual thinking tools; they contain assumptions, like every financial model. Connecting the two can lead to important insights and support decision making across the organization. For scenario planners, it is important to understand the potential benefits of what you do and to communicate that to a client organization. Bringing scenarios together with organizational financial models is a critically important way to make it clear that scenarios can instruct finance officers and prepare the organization—financially—for significant shifts in the external environment.

11 ■ Developing Scenario Signals and Critical Uncertainty Dashboards

Signals are one of the most important outcomes of scenario planning, and they should be mandatory. They are usually undervalued. Signals provide a direct feedback loop to the external environment in terms of what people see going on in the world around them and how they interpret what they see (Davis, 2003). In short, signals are the events required for a given scenario to emerge in reality (Schoemaker et al., 2013). They allow you to track what is happening in the political, social, technological, economic, and other environments and what is necessary for any given scenario to happen (Silver, 2012). While signals never perfectly align with a specific scenario, over time, reality starts to look more like one of the scenarios than the others.

For example, in a scenario project with an aerospace company that built and sent rockets into space, the signals were a valuable output. In this case, the scenario team was aware that many of their rocket engines were being manufactured in Russia. On the completion of our scenario work, one of our signals (in a specific scenario) involved the deteriorating relations between the United States and Russia. Six weeks after the conclusion of our work, the team was shocked to see the banner scrolling across the bottom of the television screen indicating that President Obama issued a ban on Russian rocket engines, with a series of additional sanctions. I immediately called my colleague at Rocket Company, and we talked about how in the prior weeks, Rocket Company had sourced another firm to provide the necessary engines. While it was still receiving engines from Russia at the time, the ability to see the signal and having already thought about an alternative allowed Rocket Company to react with lightning speed. It was able to switch to another supplier without any disruption to the supply chain.

This is an example of a specific, game-changing signal that decision makers were able to identify early and follow. In cases where *many* events in the real world map to the signals already identified for a given scenario, there is some assurance that the scenario work has described much of how things have actually turned out.

There are two important ways to think about signals. The first is the actual signals (events) required for any scenario to evolve in reality, and the second is a critical uncertainty dashboard. Both are extremely important when thinking about how to monitor the external environment and how it is changing. This chapter will demonstrate both. The purposes of using these tools are specifically to understand how the external world is changing and to monitor critical uncertainties, both of which can lead to faster decision making and action.

Signals

Once scenarios are developed, the task of deciding on signals is a careful process of reviewing the scenarios in detail and imagining the headlines that would coincide with the story contained in each scenario (Meissner et al., 2017). One approach is to break each scenario down into smaller blocks of time. If you have a set of five-year scenarios, consider breaking it into one-year intervals. What would need to happen in the first year? The second year? And so on.

	Scenario 1	Scenario 2	Scenario 3	Scenario x
Year 1 signals	List 3–5 signals here	. . .	. . .	. . .
Year 2 signals	List 3–5 signals here	. . .	. . .	. . .
Year 3 signals	List 3–5 signals here	. . .	. . .	. . .
Year 4 signals	List 3–5 signals here	. . .	. . .	. . .
Year 5 signals	List 3–5 signals here	. . .	. . .	. . .

Figure 11.1. Scenario Signals

This exercise will force people to think about what would drive a given scenario into reality. It is a common practice among scenario planners to think about the newspaper headlines or, more modernly, the banner scrolling across the bottom of any media channel (Ramirez & Wilkinson, 2016; Schwartz, 1996; van der Heijden, 2005). Signals should therefore be succinct, written like a headline snippet to get the idea across. No detailed elaboration is required, and because of this, developing signals is usually a highly creative activity, just like scenario development.

Figure 11.1 provides a simple signals template that can be adapted and changed in terms of the number of scenarios involved and the timeline of the scenario exercise.

Figure 11.1 assumes a five-year timeline for the scenarios. The figure and template can easily be adjusted for longer-term scenarios. For example, the first column could read "Year 1–2 signals," "Year 3–4 signals," and so on for a 10-year overall scenario timeline. Developing signals provides a way to understand how the world is changing and enables an understanding of whether reality is headed toward a description contained in one of the scenarios.

Example: Natural Gas Company

A recent scenario project with Natural Gas Company focused on a potential decline in demand for natural gas. The purpose of the scenarios was to explore more widely how the industry could change and what might drive a significant drop in natural gas demand. Scenarios were built using the 2×2 matrix method, and one of the key outcomes was the development of scenario signals. The signals were used (and are still being used) to track events that may have implications for the natural gas industry. While you don't have enough context to fully understand the meaning of these signals, they are provided simply as an instructive example. Figure 11.2 shows the signals for Natural Gas Company by scenario with a five-year timeline.

It should be easy to see by the headlines that this was a recent project. And some of the events have already occurred. The careful observer will also notice that the signals get more extreme as the years go by. Signals don't have to be extremely difficult work. The scenarios will obviously already include some events in the storylines. The challenge is to identify unique, more provocative events that the scenarios do not already contain. Writing them as headlines also changes the way you think about the events needed for a given scenario to actually happen.

Workshop Format and Guidelines: Developing Signals

Time: 2–4 hours.
Participants: 5–15.

Assumptions: You have a set of scenarios.

Workshop Format: There are three different ways to approach this exercise:

1. Teamwork (e.g., face-to-face, online)
2. Individual work (assigning each scenario to a different person to develop the signals)
3. Individual work (one individual is assigned the task of developing signals for all scenarios)

Instructions:

- For teamwork, assemble the team and reread and engage with scenario 1.
  - Using internet search resources, magazines, newspaper articles, and any other resources, the team works together, scenario by scenario, to identify specific events required for scenario 1.
  - The process is repeated for the remaining scenarios.
- For individual work in which each scenario is assigned to a different person:
  - Each individual does their own research and creative thinking about the events required for their assigned scenario.
  - A meeting is scheduled to report back to the team on signals. The team can then debate, add, and clarify signals to arrive at a final signals list for each scenario.
- For individual work in which one person is assigned the entire task:
  - The assigned person does their own research, creative thinking, internet searches, and develops signals for all scenarios.
  - A meeting is scheduled to report back to the team on signals. The team can then debate, add, and clarify signals to arrive at a final signals list for each scenario.

Products:

- The outcome of this activity is to have a list of event headlines for each scenario.

Signals and Strategies

Combining signals and strategies directly supports the anticipatory nature of using scenarios (Goodwin, 2019). For example, if you have developed generic strategies as described in chapter 5 and then developed signals for each scenario, putting them together allows you to anticipate. In other words, you have created a system for tracking

	Salmon Scenario	Mule Scenario	Eagle Scenario	Porcupine Scenario
Year 1 signals	• "Tariff tensions with China escalate" • "Steel strain hits Rust Belt" • "The rise of the carnivores"	• "The rise and demise of Amazon" • "Trump wins 2020" • "Trump vs. Bezos—the real election"	• "3 years after the great crash, America slowly on the road to recovery" • "Horizontal investment across America" • "Feds hope cutting interest rates will spark growth"	• "What does the Amazon attack mean for your family?" • "Cases in identity theft on the rise" • "Amazon workers strike continues to day 8"
Year 2 signals	• "Too big to fail? Too heavy to use?" • "Steel alternative start-ups on the rise" • "Is 'veganism' over?"	• "SEC approves Google's takeover of Amazon" • "Can Chi-tah play with Alibaba?" • "Trump's EPA pick loosens HAZMAT regulation"	• "Department of Transportation hosts mass hiring events" • "Hurricane Mike pummels Georgia and South Carolina" • "Non-essential spending at all-time low"	• "Walmart eyeing Amazon acquisition" • "eBay looking to win former Amazon customers" • "The rise of small business"
Year 3 signals	• "Millennials, Gen Z, and the on-demand economy" • "A portrait of America's empty main streets"	• "The unlikely partnership of Bezos and Ma" • "Chi-tah promises delivery in 30 minutes or less"	• "U.S. government buys steel futures" • "The new survival tech you need—propane!"	• "Consumer spending up as prices fall" • "Bezos's Balkanized business model"

Year 4 signals	• "Bread consumption linked to cancer risk" • "Temperatures set to break heat records again this summer" • "Why your doctor is telling you to eat steak" • "Understanding Steelite, the renewable steel"	• "How to identify a self-driving car on the highway" • "Millennials are killing big brands" • "Chi-tah can predict your next order better than you can" • "Millennials and Gen Z prefer cooking at home"	• "3D printing steel replacements on the rise" • "Companies using technology to lure back customers" • "Meeting consumers where they are, one company's journey" • "Recession statistics—American's dine out less"	• "After taking over the Midwest, BITE sets sights on the South" • "BITE, the app you've never heard of and need to download" • "Direct to consumer delivery on the rise" • "Will Americans embrace Alibaba?"
Year 5 signals	• "Scientists turn compost into steel alternative" • "Are carbs killing Americans?" • "Amazon selling 3D printers direct to consumers"	• "Influencers getting into the cooking game" • "Your house knows when you're out of milk"	• "FEMA will stay in Georgia and South Carolina for 2 more years" • "Solar and extractive—how to integrate power" • "Did IoT save this family from Hurricane Mike's destruction?"	• "Subscription addiction—have you tried a subscription box yet?" • "BITE-mobiles coming to a town near you"

Figure 11.2. Natural Gas Company Signals

Scenario 1		Scenario 2		Scenario 3		Scenario 4	
Signals	Generic Strategies	Signals	Generic Strategies	Signals	Generic Strategies	Signals	Generic Strategies
• Signal 1	• Strategy 1	• Signal 1	• Strategy 1	• Signal 1	• Strategy 1	• Signal 1	• Strategy 1
• Signal 2	• Strategy 2	• Signal 2	• Strategy 2	• Signal 2	• Strategy 2	• Signal 2	• Strategy 2
• Signal 3	• Strategy 3	• Signal 3	• Strategy 3	• Signal 3	• Strategy 3	• Signal 3	• Strategy 3
Etc.	Etc.	Etc.	Etc.	Etc.	Etc.	Etc.	Etc.

Figure 11.3. Combining Signals and Strategies

the external environment, and, having already thought through relevant actions or strategies, you can react faster. A template for combining signals and strategies is provided in figure 11.3.

This tool allows users to consider each scenario, one at a time, and understand that if a group of signals that align with a certain scenario collect over time, they already know what to do. It allows people to get ahead of the competition. In other words, if you see a collection of signals that strongly suggests Scenario 2 is happening, you have already thought about action. Combining signals and strategies is like a simplified contingency plan: strategies are identified for each scenario, and in time, the signals will tend to show which scenario is happening.

Example: Natural Gas Company

Sticking with the Natural Gas Company example, the signals were combined with the generic strategies that were previously identified (following the exercise in chapter 5). Again, combining the outputs of these two exercises creates a powerful tool that provides you with the ability to react faster and be more agile than other companies. For purposes of simplicity and elegance, the signals and strategy example shows the product for only one scenario (you would do the same for the other three). See figure 11.4.

The signals and strategies for Natural Gas Company are currently being used to understand how the environment is changing, and

Salmon Scenario	
Signals	Strategies
Over time, if we see events or "headlines:" like these . . .	. . . We should consider these strategies
• "Tariff tensions with China escalate" • "Steel strain hits Rust Belt?" • "The rise of the carnivores" • Too big to fail? Too heavy to use!" • "Steel alternative start-ups on the rise" • "Is 'veganism' over?" • "Millennials, Gen-Z, and the on-demand economy" • "A portrait of America's empty main streets" • "Bread consumption linked to cancer risk" • Temperatures set to break heat records again this summer" • "Why your doctor is telling you to eat steak" • "Understanding Steelite, the renewable steel" • "Scientists turn compost into steel alternative" • "Are carbs killing American?" • "Amazon selling 3D printers direct to consumers"	• Tank innovation drives down the cost of product • Tank innovation for multiple uses • Tank innovation to remove dependency on raw materials • Consumer awareness marketing campaign for delivery options • Acquisition growth in areas lacking coverage • Production innovation to support new tank design • Production innovation to support speed and lower cost • Delivery driver assistance • Vehicle innovation for efficient delivery • IoT for tank • Smart self-serve options (vending) • Direct to consumer distribution • Partner-based distribution • International expansion

Figure 11.4. Signal and Strategies for Natural Gas Company

they are reviewed every two weeks as part of the strategy meeting for the organization. Not a lot of time is spent on this—about 15 minutes is allocated to looking through the signals and asking the team if these headlines (or similar) are appearing.

Workshop Format and Guidelines: Signals and Strategies

This is not really a workshop (although it could be done that way). If you have done the work of identifying signals and you have the outputs of using scenarios described in previous chapters (i.e., generic strategies, opportunities and threats), it is simply a matter of putting them together. Usually this is done in a document or slide to be frequently reviewed by the scenario team and relevant decision makers.

Signals Summary

Signals are a critically important part of using scenarios. As this section has demonstrated, signals can be used on their own as a way to stay on top of changes in the external environment. They can be paired with strategies as shown in the Natural Gas Company case. Signals can also be used with any of the other exercises described in this book. For example, consider the previous chapter on scenarios and financial models; you could use signals to help understand which scenario may be emerging and the implications for organizational revenue and costs. This activity creates the ability to change course quickly once you understand how the world is changing. When using signals with financial models, you might be able to make cost-saving decisions or, if possible, develop new potential revenue sources if you are in a scenario that demands it. If you have been able to complete most or all of the scenario uses described in this book, signals can allow you to understand which strategies to seriously consider, which decisions to take, how to adjust organizational revenue expectations, and generally how to react much faster than your competition.

Critical Uncertainty Dashboards

In most cases of scenario planning there are a reasonable number of critical uncertainties that become the frames or drivers of the scenario plots. This is true regardless of the scenario development method used. These are the factors that could potentially require a serious shift to the business, and there is knowledge of how these factors will play out. No matter the process used to develop scenarios, there is always a category of things that are highly uncertain that could change the industry or the organization's business model fundamentally. However, there are some cases when there is a longer-than-usual list of critical uncertainties. Choosing a few to frame a set of scenarios can leave a lot of uncertainty on the table. When there is an extensive list of critical uncertainties, it can easily lead to too many scenarios or a loss of complexity. In situations like this, a useful solution is to consider a critical uncertainty dashboard.

The point of this dashboard is to make a listing of all the critical uncertainties and create a system to track them. Using a simple table, you can list the uncertainty, create a column for the observed trend of that uncertainty, and create another column for data supporting the trend (see figure 11.5).

Example: Medical Device Company

Critical uncertainty dashboards are commonly used when the current situation is highly uncertain and involves many changing elements. As an example, a medical device company used a critical uncertainty dashboard in April 2020, when it became obvious that the COVID-19 pandemic was going to be a problem. Participants were led through the initial stages of scenario planning intending

Critical Uncertainty	Trend	Data
Critical uncertainty 1		
Critical uncertainty 2		
Critical uncertainty 3		
Critical uncertainty 4		
Etc.		

Figure 11.5. Critical Uncertainty Dashboard Template

to arrive at a 2 × 2 matrix. Brainstorming, categorizing, impact rank-ing, and uncertainty ranking workshops were all facilitated (see chapter 3 for more details). Once the rankings were complete, the team was overwhelmed by how many forces fell into the "high impact / high uncertainty" box of the ranking space. Going further in developing and writing scenarios was abandoned.

In this case we developed a critical uncertainty dashboard to keep track of the major elements associated with the COVID-19 pandemic. Because the number of critical uncertainties was so high, it made sense to skip developing scenarios and rely on the dashboard to under-stand how the external environment was changing instead of the usual longer-term thinking required in developing scenarios. The COVID situation had already arrived, and the large number of uncer-tainties were all related to understanding its impact (see figure 11.6).

Another important reason for skipping the development of sce-narios was the fact that the purpose of development scenarios was no longer relevant. Remember that scenarios work best when trying to understand what the *next* potential crisis (or significant industry shift) could be over a longer time frame. In highly unstable situa-tions when a crisis or major shift is already under way, the outlook is shorter (one to two years) and the focus becomes managing through the short-term effects. In these situations, scenarios lose value.

Workshop Format and Guidelines: Creating a Critical Uncer-tainty Dashboard

Time: 2–4 hours.
Participants: 5–15.

Assumptions:

- You have identified an overwhelming list of critical uncertainties.
- Proceeding with developing scenarios carries a high risk of losing too much complexity.
- The situation involves events that have already occurred and requires shorter-term attention to solutions that scenarios can't provide.

Uncertainty	Trend	Data
Availability and recording of testing	2.5% to 28.4%	Between 808K and 9.4M of 330M people in the United States have been tested. Test availability is increasing.
Timeline for pandemic resolution	6 to 12 months	Declining infection rates in most states, increasing antibody test availability, and a phased reopening.
Successful vaccine development	Human trials	More than 90 vaccines are in development and 6 have moved into human trials. Testing is inconclusive.
Availability and cost of proximity tracking devices	Widely available	Many reasonably priced solutions are capable of outdoor and indoor movement tracking. Fewer are able to account for rooms/walls.
Antibody testing	Accuracy unproven	Test accuracy is <u>inconclusive</u> and availability is scattered. Test validation is under way.
COVID-19-related bankruptcy	In development	Cities and counties are projected to lose billions in tax revenue. Private sector profits are decreasing. Impacts are coming to fruition.
Rise/decline in cases	Moderate	Overall U.S. daily infection rates are plateauing. Some states that reopened early are seeing a rise in infections.
Unemployment	Sharply increasing	Unemployment filings are sharply increasing and projected to grow.

No concern ▪ Moderate concern ■ Significant concern

Figure 11.6. Critical Uncertainty Dashboard for Medical Device Company

Workshop Format: This exercise can be done as a team or individually. Either way, the instructions are the same.

Instructions:

- List the critical uncertainties.
- Identify the data that will be used to track how each critical uncertainty will evolve.

- Identify the current information and trend on each critical uncertainty.
- As appropriate, color-code the "trend" column according to whether the trend is moving in a negative (red) or positive (green) direction or is holding steady (yellow).

Summary

In this chapter, two important tools for following changes in the external environment have been described. At first glance, using these tools may appear to be simple, yet to use them properly and effectively requires dedication and commitment over time. Practice with these tools naturally creates a higher likelihood that the scenario effort will be sustained—someone should be tracking the signals or uncertainties on the dashboard. Disciplined attention to these tools may define a path to help embed scenario planning into the organizational culture, which is the focus of chapter 12.

12 ■ Making Scenarios a Part of Organizational Culture

One of the greatest mysteries of scenarios is why they have not been widely adopted as a standard organizational practice. After 50 years, the most commonly referenced organization when it comes to scenarios is still Shell. There is a good reason for this: over half a century, Shell remains the only organization with a consistent, ongoing, and public production of scenarios for the energy industry. Getting scenarios adopted and embedded into the organizational culture remains a difficult task—so difficult, in fact, that there is an N of 1, with a successful long-term scenario tradition. For sure, building scenarios into the organizational culture continues to be a challenge for scenario planners.

As the saying goes, culture eats strategy for breakfast (see, e.g., Teasdale, 2002; Whitzman, 2016). The tools in this book are aimed at helping culture and strategy eat breakfast together. The majority of scenario projects are one-off activities. In most cases, a lack of purpose, a lack of guidance on how to use scenarios, and a lack of connection to measurable outcomes are the reasons why. Yet strategic planning enjoys real popularity without consistent evidence of performance or utility. What is the difference?

Scenario planning generally requires more time, effort, and energy than traditional strategic and business planning. Chapter 2 should have made it clear that strategic and business planning approaches are commonly based on old tools that don't require deep thinking to complete. They don't often lead to real insights about the industry or environment, and they are usually vague and shallow. Good scenarios require creative thinking, extensive research, and internal consistency to achieve. All of this takes time. And then, you have to use them. Putting all of this together means scenarios need to become an ongoing effort. Scenarios simply cannot be developed and used to make strategic decisions in an annual one- or two-day workshop. These key differences make it more difficult to embed scenario planning as a standard organizational process and, therefore, part of organizational culture.

There are ways to overcome these difficulties, and this chapter describes how. The four main ways of making scenarios a part of organizational culture are (1) prioritizing signals, (2) using scenarios (going beyond thinking tools), (3) showing the financial impact of scenarios, and (4) requiring that decisions and budget requests be justified through scenarios. Prioritizing signals is important because it means someone has to be assigned to track the signals and observe how the environment is changing. This activity automatically keeps scenarios alive as it requires ongoing attention to the scenarios and events in reality. Generating and testing strategies and decisions forces a deeper analysis of what actions are available and how they might perform in different situations. This usually leads to more resilient actions that allow leaders to avoid being blindsided. Assessing the financial benefits of scenarios creates the business case for their use and can trace the outcomes of decisions back to the scenario exercise. Finally, the main reason Shell has established a culture of scenarios for over 50 years is because managers are expected to justify their decisions and budget requests through scenarios.

Collectively using these four strategies provides the best chance of making scenarios a part of organizational culture. Before getting to the practical utility of this chapter, it is important to review some foundational concepts that lay the groundwork for the recommendations that follow. First, organizational culture is briefly defined and described. Then, two theoretical concepts from the scenario planning literature are reviewed: (1) shared mental models and (2) the strategic conversation. These ideas create a basis for how to think about scenarios as part of organizational culture and what that could look like. The purposes of this chapter are the following:

1. Define and describe organizational culture
2. Describe shared mental models
3. Describe the "strategic conversation" as a part of organizational culture
4. Provide practical recommendations for making scenarios part of organizational culture

What Is Organizational Culture?

Organizational culture is a concept that has been borrowed from anthropology and applied in the organizational sciences. There is little agreement in either discipline about exactly what the term "culture" means because it is a fluid concept. For the purposes of this chapter, organizational culture is "the basic assumptions and beliefs that are shared by members of an organization that operate unconsciously, and that define a basic 'taken-for-granted fashion' an organization's view of itself and its environment" (Schein, 1985, pp. 6–7).

Culture is both a set of data (values, ideals, beliefs, and experiences) and the procedures that allow for what to do with the data. Cultural processes rely on informational databases built of input, values, assumptions, and tools (Bohannan, 1995). These informational databases, along with a set of procedures, can create a shared mental model of a group's culture. They are also the shared mental model that creates the cultural process. Because of how these are connected, it is clear that any changes to the shared mental model of the group could have an impact on the culture of the group. Stated simply, organizational culture is a moving concept based on both the values and beliefs held within an organization and the processes used to communicate them across the organization. Practically, organizational culture is how things get done. It is the standard set of general organizational practices that members accept.

Shared Mental Models

Before diving into shared mental models, it is important to understand the concept of individual mental models. In short, your mental model is the way you see the world. It is built on your experiences (successes and failures) and generally directs how you see the world. Is it a place of happiness and opportunity? Is it a place of suffering and challenge? Is it something in between? Some of this is a function of how you grew up, and there is no question that childhood experiences shape later belief systems—mental models. While these concepts may seem far away from scenario planning (and this is not a book about psychotherapy), your view of the world has a definite influence on how you think about your organization and the decisions you make. Mental models are critically important in scenario planning because they influence how you view your industry, organization, and coworkers, and what you think is possible as the future unfolds. One purpose of scenarios is to break your mental model by creating something that is shared. Exposure to other mental models through dialogue is how scenarios can help you learn to see the world from other perspectives. The point is to think together, rather than individually or separately. Through exposure to other people's mental models, part of the scenario process is to create awareness that all mental models are limited. There is no complete, true, and accurate mental model of the world, organization, business unit, work team, or other.

Shared mental models have long been a part of the scenario planning literature (van der Heijden, 1996, 2005, 2011). Shared mental models are "a wide range of initially unstructured thoughts and views, and out of this create shared interpretations of the world in which the majority of the individual insights can find a logical place" (van der Heijden, 1996, p. 42). Shared mental models create the organizational dialogue through which individuals can analyze, share, and rebuild their mental models and open their minds to new possibilities. "If action is based on planning on the basis of a mental model, then institutional action must be based on a shared mental model. Through conversation elements of observation and thought can be structured and embedded in the accepted and shared organizational theories-in-use" (van der Heijden, 1996, p. 41). When groups of people have common experiences, the result is often a shared understanding of the situation. Scenarios enable these groups to negotiate and come to agreement on the primary features of the environment and to develop actions that can be taken. Putting these elements together allows groups to build what is called a strategic conversation.

The Strategic Conversation

Based on building some degree of a shared mental model across the organization—or at least the leadership team—an ongoing conversation about strategy and alternatives is called a strategic conversation. The simple idea is that scenarios and strategy have to be more than an annual meeting. Scenarios and strategy have to become a part of the normal, ongoing conversation that takes place within an organization. When this is achieved, you can keep scenarios alive through conversation. If action is based on planning with an individual mental model, institutional action has to be based on a shared mental model. A process of dialogue can lead to elements of observation and thought that are used to continually review strategy options (van der Heijden, 1996, p. 41). An effective strategic conversation requires four parts: (1) a common language, (2) alignment of ideas, (3) willingness to engage in rational argumentation, and (4) the evolution of ideas inside the organization (van der Heijden, 1996).

Common Language

The requirement for common language is logical and not complex. Stated simply, organization members involved in any organizational process need a common understanding. People have to define and sort through the jargon that has invaded today's business world. Participation in a scenario process allows for the negotiation of a shared language. Participants come to an understanding about what scenarios are and how they can be used to help support strategy and decision making.

Alignment of Ideas

Strategy literature increasingly includes reference to the notion of alignment (Manning, 2002; Mintzberg & Lampel, 1999). While most of the strategy literature refers to alignment among organization, process, and individual goals, the strategic conversation aims to produce alignment among ideas. The strategic conversation stresses the importance of identifying and analyzing assumptions. In scenario planning, idea alignment becomes an output of building a collective mental model (Wack, 1985a, 1985b, 1985c). Sharing assumptions, values, and the basic parts of a unified purpose is critical to establishing this kind of alignment (Manning, 2002).

Willingness to Engage in Rational Argumentation

Scenarios raise different points of view. They are supposed to be provocative. Scenarios are often based on dialogue, participant ability to challenge each other, and a willingness to critique ideas. Participants have to be able to engage in debate, and they must be open to having their ideas challenged by others. Learning happens when people begin to see things in new or different ways, and scenarios are one way to make this happen. Without real disagreement, debate, and dialogue, the scenario process is not able to reach its full potential. This is why diversity of thought and point of view is so critical in using scenarios.

Evolution of Ideas inside the Organization

This final part of the strategic conversation is an outcome of the previous three. The evolution of ideas in the organization is the goal of the strategic conversation. It is set by developing a common language, working toward aligning ideas, and being willing to critique and be

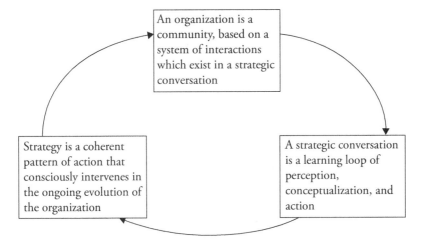

Figure 12.1. The Art of Strategic Conversation (van der Heijden, 1996, p. 274)

critiqued by other people in an organization. Often, scenarios are just a starting point for sparking ideas, which leads to revision of the scenarios and further debate and dialogue until assumptions are shattered. Once you start using scenarios, the language, alignment of ideas, and critique all continue as input into decision making and strategy.

The parts of a strategic conversation are intended to clarify what it takes to achieve this kind of ongoing strategy dialogue. It is essential for real insights and innovation. The parts of the strategic conversation are logically built into scenario planning—particularly when the scenarios are used (figure 12.1).

Making Scenarios a Part of Organizational Culture

Having established these foundational concepts, there are four ways to think about how to make scenarios a part of organizational culture:

- Prioritizing signals
- Using the tools described in this book to generate and test strategies and decisions

- Assessing how scenarios can have a financial benefit and ultimately affect the organizational financial model
- Having leadership require that scenarios be used to justify decisions and budget requests

Prioritizing Signals

The first way to make scenarios a part of organizational culture is to use signals. Signals are developed toward the end of the scenario process, and when done well (and assigned to an individual or team to track), they create further attention to scenarios. They keep the scenarios alive. The most common recommendation I make to my own clients is to start the monthly leadership team meeting with a brief review of the signals.

Using Scenarios

The entire premise of this book is that using scenarios is the most important way to advance the field. At risk of belaboring the point, scenario planners have not done a good job of making sure their scenarios are used to achieve outcomes. It is no wonder that scenarios have not been widely adopted. Scenarios can be an exciting experience that stretches the thinking inside the organization and literally changes how people think about the future (Lew et al., 2019). But that is not enough. Scenarios need to be connected to decisions and actions. *Using Scenarios* has shown seven different ways of putting scenarios into action. Simply applying the tools provided in this book will be a benefit. You don't have to use them all, and you don't have to make it complicated. Starting with some of the more simple tools in chapters 5, 6, and 7 will be enough to start putting your scenarios into action.

Assessing the Financial Benefit of Scenarios

Organizational activities that do not carry an estimate or analysis of financial benefit ultimately wind up being something "nice to do." This cannot be the fate of scenario planning. The importance of assessing the financial benefits of scenarios (or at least estimating them) cannot be overstated. Because scenario work has never been connected to financial assessment, this area is ripe for development. This book has suggested two different ways to consider the financial benefits of scenarios and to understand the impact of scenarios on the organizational financial model. These activities should become a standard practice, and they need to be applied in order to advance the field and improve organizations.

Making Scenarios a Requirement

This is not a book about leadership, but the role of leaders cannot be denied. How many times have you experienced a leader who finds a book, promptly orders copies for every employee, and makes it required reading? Something as simple as a book is commonly directed from the top down and usually it is a fable, like *Who Moved My Cheese?* Leaders should demand that scenarios be used to assess decision making. Requiring managers to justify decisions and budget requests through a set of scenarios means making scenarios a routine part of how people operate—the very definition of organizational culture.

Summary

This chapter has described the concept of organizational culture and the related scenario ideas of shared mental models and the strategic conversation. While these ideas have generally been in the theoretical realm, the suggestions and recommendations made in this chapter bring them into the practical realm. Most newcomers to scenario planning ask why scenarios are not being used by every company, and the response is usually silence.

13 ▪ Advancing Scenario and Strategic Planning

The road from scenarios to strategy is not always clear. The thoughtful work of using scenarios in different ways and connecting them to strategy promises to be rewarding and beneficial for both scenarios and strategy. To reiterate, the fundamental purpose of this book is to provide practical guidance on how to use and apply scenarios for improving organizations. In doing so, scenarios need to be connected to strategy. Serious scenario and strategy professionals will tell you that scenarios need to be put to use in order to have a positive impact on organizations. Being mindful about the purpose of scenarios and making sure they have an influence on strategic decision making is essential to success. Simply stated, making sure scenarios get used is the most direct path to solving the utility problems with strategic planning in improving organizations.

This book has reviewed the major problems with the practices of both strategic and scenario planning. Again, scenarios should open up thinking for putting strategy into action. Each realm of practice often is lacking: scenarios lack a connection to action, and strategy lacks up-front analysis of multiple futures. Putting the two together in an integrated way is required, and this book provides a method for doing so. To briefly review, strategic planning has suffered from being addicted to a prediction mentality—separating strategy development and implementation. For example, situating strategy within the finance team and blindly applying strategies that worked for similar companies is a formula for failure. On the scenario planning side, the field has primarily been held back by a lack of guidance on how to actually use scenarios.

A Review of the Different Ways to Use Scenarios

Using Scenarios addresses many of these problems head-on. Specifically related to strategic planning, this book provides the tools to solve the prediction mentality, address the thinking/doing gap, and call out the practice of selecting a high-profile strategy that worked for a famous company. More specifically, for scenario planning, the main focus has been to describe alternative ways to use scenarios. To review, the seven different approaches to using scenarios are as follows:

1. Connecting scenarios to a purpose
2. Generating strategies
3. Creating and stress-testing strategic plans with scenarios
4. Testing decisions and options with scenarios
5. Assessing the financial benefits of scenarios
6. Modeling financials with scenarios
7. Developing scenario signals and critical uncertainty dashboards

Each of these approaches has been described in detail in this book. Templates, examples, and workshop instructions have also been included. You should be able to apply any of these approaches following the guidance offered. Of course, the exercises and interventions become more comfortable with practice. The tools provided in this book are meant to help put scenarios into action. In order for scenario

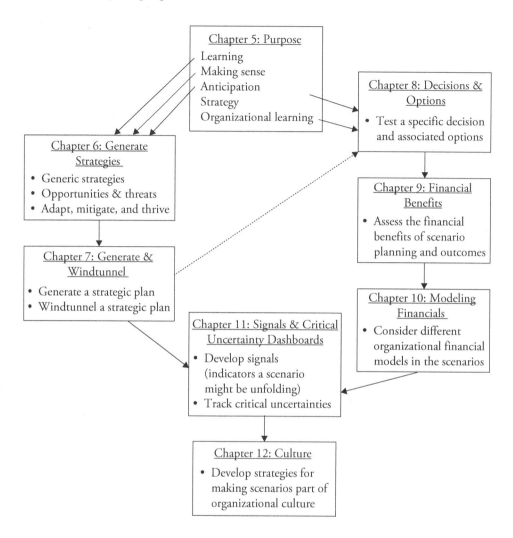

Figure 13.1. Overall Process for Using Scenarios

planning and strategic planning to be advanced, they need to work together.

This book is intended for people who have created a set of scenarios and want to know what to do with them. If you are new to using scenarios, pick an approach and try it out. One factor to keep in mind is that being capable of using all of the approaches in this book provides a way to make scenarios a part of organizational culture and help them become a standard organizational practice. Once again, figure 13.1 illustrates the seven approaches to using scenarios and how they are related, with an ultimate goal of embedding scenarios in the organization.

Conclusion

This book is intended to fill a gap. Going beyond interesting stories is critical to achieve widespread adoption of scenarios. Continuing to be vague about what to do after you have scenarios will only keep holding the field back. The alternative is a field that opens up with opportunities to develop more and different ways to use scenarios. This is the thriving and vibrant field that will make scenarios a whole practice. Scenarios and strategy should be the most important organizational activities. The follow-up on scenarios that explore multiple futures addresses how they can be used to have an impact in practice.

This book has described seven different ways you can use your scenarios. From creative thinking to detailed financial analyses—descriptions, examples, and workshop guidelines have been provided. Yet, these are only the beginning. My hope is that this book, while provocative in places, encourages others in the field to respond with additional ways of using scenarios that are not described here. The single greatest opportunity for advancing scenario planning is to be specific about how they can be used and what they can help decision makers achieve. It is in this realm that we have failed. To be sure, tools that go beyond interesting stories about the future that can connect those interesting stories to action are needed.

A focus on applying and using scenarios is the surest way to advance scenario planning practices and connect scenarios to action and outcomes. Without this, scenarios will likely remain a one-off activity. Instead, the goal is to make scenarios a standard practice that is widely used and just as common as strategic planning. In order to achieve that goal, scenarios have to be used and their value must be clear. This book has provided a first step in that direction. For those interested in advancing the field, I hope the tools I have described are helpful in demonstrating the value of scenario planning. Further, I hope to provoke other ideas about how to use scenarios. All of this is aimed at helping decision makers and leaders cope with a constantly changing future.

Afterword

The proposal for *Using Scenarios* was approved by Berrett-Koehler in March 2020. Because of the time during which this was written, COVID-19 deserves special attention. While I have referred to the pandemic several times throughout these pages, it requires some discussion as I completed the book in December 2020, and with revisions into the spring and summer of 2021.

The Most Difficult Barrier for Scenarios

It is without question that events will arise that were seemingly not anticipated at all. Yet, history shows that some events were predicted by people who were not listened to. Any current or future book about scenarios cannot avoid the case of COVID-19. Bill Gates foresaw and warned of the coming pandemic almost a decade before it happened. Other infectious disease experts also made their warnings long before the pandemic arrived. It is impossible to deny these facts, and the strongest governments in the world ignored the signs. I am re-minded of a story told by Pierre Wack to Arie de Geus back in the Shell days. De Geus adjusted the story when he published it in 1992:

> In this story, the listener is invited to assume that a person with absolute powers to predict the future is visiting the Mayor of Rotterdam in 1920. The visitor tells the Mayor in vivid detail what is going to happen to his town and its German hinterland over the next 25 years (the period covered by a scenario!). It is thus, during an otherwise perfectly normal working day in 1920 that the Mayor hears about the advent of the Republic of Wei-mar, about hyper-inflation, the crash of the stock exchange in 1929 followed by the Great Depression, the rise of Nazism in Germany with its (for Rotterdam) damaging economic poli-cies of autarchy, the outbreak of the 2nd World War with the carpet-bombing of his town's whole city centre and, finally, the systematic destruction of the town's port installations during the calamitous winter of 1945.
>
> The question is: what does the reader think that the Mayor is going to do with this information which reaches him in 1920, amidst all the other opinions and facts which he hears in the course of executing his complicated task of running one of the world's biggest ports?
>
> The quasi-unanimous reply which I receive to this rhetori-cal question is—*nothing*—even if our Mayor would give this prediction a higher degree of credibility than much of the other information reaching him, he would neither have the courage nor the powers of persuasion necessary to take the far reach-ing decisions required by this prediction.
>
> *The future cannot be predicted and, even if it could, we would not dare to act on the prediction.* (de Geus, 1992, p. 2)

Thus, it remains one of the most perplexing problems of sce-nario planning: If your worst fears are revealed in a set of scenar-ios, do you really have the courage to consider the effects and what you will do under those circumstances? The answer over history is probably not, because you will not really believe it; and even if you do, you will not have the powers of persuasion required to convince others.

Scenario Timelines and Focus

As the pandemic worsened into the spring of 2021, there was a flurry of scenario activity by a variety of consulting firms. All of the pandemic scenarios available at the time of this writing are based on the 2 × 2 matrix method, and almost all of them use "severity of the pandemic" and "timeline of the pandemic" as the axes on their matrices. While scenarios can certainly be developed for the short term, this activity misses the point. Scenarios were originally meant to think about the long term. Careful observers will see that scenarios are best used to identify the next crisis, not to deal with the one that is already here. The real power of scenarios lies in looking a bit further ahead. COVID-19 arrived, and we had to manage the effects the best we could. Scenarios are not the best answer to short-term crises. There are other tools for that. Scenarios, as they were originally intended, are to look ahead, to see the next crisis, to wonder what might blindside us, our company, or our globe in the future.

Scenario timelines continue to increase in variety. It is common to see 5-, 10-, 15-, 20-, and even 50-year scenarios. Scenarios are also being created in increasingly diverse realms with wildly different scopes (e.g., climate change, forest management, corporate strategy, the global energy industry, city planning, transportation planning, among many others). It is important to recognize that as scenarios expand with timelines and increase in scope, the ability to use them declines. For example, 50-year global energy industry scenarios will not be useful for decision making. This is because every region, country, state, city, and community will have different critical dynamics to deal with, and the decisions they have available are significantly different. This is the very reason why the global COVID-19 scenarios are not very useful.

In my example with Healthcare Company in chapter 10, we abandoned the scenario process because we recognized that the pandemic was already here and that creating scenarios was not the best approach. If you recall, we instead created a critical uncertainty dashboard to track the critical uncertainties of virus spread, vaccine developments, infection rates, testing rates, and others. This allowed decision makers to understand developments in the environment (in the short term) and anticipate the implications for their organization. To emphasize the point, careful consideration of the timeline and scope of scenarios has real implications for how to use them.

Sometimes Close Is Close Enough

Scenarios often capture events that never happen. Sometimes, though, they contain events that have implications that are almost identical to those of the events that actually occur. For example, the scenarios we produced in January 2019 for Healthcare Company contained some unique events. While the scenarios did not include a pandemic, one of them did include a volcano erupting. Through applying the ideas presented in this book we identified a heavy strain on the hospital system and on ICU bed capacity, as well as an immediate need for more trained health-care workers. What is the point?

While we did not have the cause exactly right, at least one of our scenarios suggested a situation not very different from the outcomes of COVID-19. To be sure, these are not the same, and had we included a pandemic in our scenarios, we could say we had it "right." Even so, we described a situation that produced very similar outcomes. This is why sometimes close is close enough, but you have to pay attention. Because of the scenarios, Healthcare Company had already taken inventory of personal protective equipment for local hospitals and began increasing their supply.

Reflection

No one, and I mean no one, can predict the future. I don't know what will happen with the pandemic or climate change. Scenarios are the closest we can come to understanding how the environment could change, and strategy provides the tools to face the fact that actions have to be taken and decisions have to be made. The contents of this book are an effort to bring the two together in complementary ways. The exercises and workshops described are intended to integrate the two. It is my hope that better integration of strategic and scenario planning (perhaps using the tools in this contribution) can improve the communities we live in and the organizations in which we work. With a little luck, we can do a better job of anticipating events that cause harm or disruption and focus attention on longer-term, more sustainable decision making.

PhD Programs

Country	University	Department	Program
Australia	University of Technology Sydney	Institute for Sustainable Futures	Doctor of Philosophy in futures studies
Colombia	Universidad Externado de Colombia (Externado University of Colombia)	Business Administration	Doctorate in Administration
Denmark	Aarhus University	School of Business and Social Sciences	Doctor of Philosophy in organizational future orientation or corporate foresight
Finland	Turun yliopisto (University of Turku)	Turku School of Economics: Finland Futures Research Centre	Doctor of Science in economics and business administration or Doctor of Philosophy—futures studies as a major

(*continued*)

Country	University	Department	Program
France	Conservatoire national des arts et métiers (CNAM) (National Conservatory of Arts and Crafts)	EPN Innovation	Doctor of Management Sciences (PhD) in foresight (prospective) management, innovation, strategy, organization
Hungary	Budapesti Corvinus Egyetem (Corvinus University of Budapest)	Doctoral School of Economic Informatics: Department of Futures Studies	Doctor of Philosophy in future research
India	University of Kerala	Faculty of Applied Science and Technology: Department of Futures Studies	Doctor of Philosophy in future studies
Iran	University of Isfahan	Department of Futures Studies	Master of Futures Studies
South Africa	University of Stellenbosch Business School (USB)	Institute of Futures Research (IFR)	Doctor of Philosophy in futures studies
UK	University of Strathclyde	Strathclyde Business School: Department of Strategy & Organisation	Doctor of Philosophy or Doctor of Business Administration in scenario thinking and scenario planning
USA	University of Hawaii at Manoa	College of Social Sciences	Doctor of Philosophy in political science with a focus on alternative futures
USA	Regent University	School of Business & Leadership	Doctor of Strategic Leadership in strategic foresight

Master's Programs

Country	University	Department	Program
Argentina	Universidad de Ciencias Empresariales y Sociales (UCES) (University of Business and Social Sciences)	Postgraduate Department	Specialization in strategic foresight
Canada	Ontario College of Art and Design University (OCAD U)	n/a	Master of Design in strategic foresight and innovation
Colombia	Institución Universitaria de Envigado (University Institution of Envigado)	Faculty of Social Sciences	Master of Psychology with a specialization in technological foresight (Prospectiva Tecnológica)
Colombia	Universidad Externado de Colombia (Externado University of Colombia)	Business Administration	Master's in strategic thinking and foresight (prospectiva)
Colombia	Universidad Pontificia Bolivariana (Pontifical Bolivarian University)	n/a	Specialization in management strategy and foresight (prospectiva)
Colombia	Universidad Tecnológica de Bolívar (Technological University of Bolívar)	n/a	Specialization in strategic planning and foresight (prospectiva)

(*continued*)

Country	University	Department	Program
Finland	Turun yliopisto (University of Turku)	Turku School of Economics: Finland Futures Research Centre	Master of Arts in futures studies
France	Conservatoire national des arts et métiers (CNAM) (National Conservatory of Arts and Crafts)	EPN Innovation	Master of Law, Economics and Management in foresight (prospective), innovation and public management (Master of Public Innovation)
France	Conservatoire national des arts et métiers (CNAM) (National Conservatory of Arts and Crafts)	EPN Innovation	Master of Law, Economics and Management in foresight (prospective), innovation and transformation of organizations
France	University of Angers	n/a	Master of Science in foresight and innovation
Germany	Freie Universität Berlin (Free University of Berlin)	Department of Education and Psychology: Institut Futur	Master of Arts in futures studies
Germany	Fachhochschule Potsdam University of Applied Sciences	Institute for Applied Research Urban Future	Master's in Urban Futures

Country	University	Department	Program
Hungary	Budapesti Corvinus Egyetem (Corvinus University of Budapest)	School of Information Economics: Economic Geography, Geoeconomics and Sustainable Development Institute: Department of Futures Studies	Master of Science in economics, regional, and environmental economics
India	University of Kerala	Faculty of Applied Science and Technology: Department of Futures Studies	Master of Philosophy in futures studies
Italy	Università di Trento (University of Trento)	Department of Sociology and Social Research	Master of Social Foresight
Mexico	CENTRO	n/a	Specialization in design of tomorrow: scenarios and solutions
Mexico	Instituto Tecnológico y de Estudios Superiores de Monterrey (Monterrey Institute of Technology and Higher Education)	School of Government and Public Transformation	Master's in strategic foresight (prospectiva)

(*continued*)

Country	University	Department	Program
Peru	Center for Higher National Studies	n/a	Master's in strategic foresight (prospectiva)
South Africa	University of Stellenbosch Business School (USB)	Institute of Futures Research	Master of Philosophy in futures studies
Taiwan	Tamkang University	College of Education: Graduate Institute of Futures Studies	Master of Education in futures studies
UK	University of Strathclyde	Strathclyde Business School: Department of Strategy & Organisation	Master of Philosophy in scenario thinking and scenario planning
USA	University of Hawaii at Manoa	College of Social Sciences	Master of Arts in alternative futures
USA	University of Houston	College of Technology	Master of Science in foresight

Undergraduate Programs

Country	University	Department	Program
Hungary	Budapesti Corvinus Egyetem (Corvinus University of Budapest)	School of Information Economics: Economic Geography, Geoeconomics and Sustainable Development Institute: Department of Futures Studies	Bachelor of Arts in future research
USA	San Diego City College	n/a	Associates in futures studies
USA	University of Hawaii at Manoa	College of Social Sciences	Bachelor of Arts in interdisciplinary studies

Short Courses

Country	University	Department	Program
Australia	Swinburne University of Technology	n/a	Graduate Certificate of Design Strategy and Innovation
Australia	University of Melbourne	Melbourne Business School	Futures Thinking and Strategy Development Program
Denmark	Aarhus University	School of Business and Social Sciences	Strategic Foresight

(*continued*)

Country	University	Department	Program
France	Conservatoire national des arts et métiers (CNAM) (National Conservatory of Arts and Crafts)	EPN Innovation	Certificate of Competence in foresight (prospective) and strategic management
France	Conservatoire national des arts et métiers (CNAM) (National Conservatory of Arts and Crafts)	EPN Innovation	Certificate of Competence in organization strategy and applied foresight
Germany	European Business School (EBS)	n/a	Module on Strategy, Corporate Foresight & Business Model Innovation in the Mobility Sector
Germany	European Business School (EBS)	n/a	Module on Strategic Foresight
Portugal	Instituto para o Desenvolvimento e Estudos Económicos, Financeiros e Empresariais (IDEFE) (Institute for Development and Economical, Financial, and Entrepreneurial Studies)	n/a	Executive Education Program: Futures, Strategic Design & Innovation

Country	University	Department	Program
Sweden	International Certified Future Strategist (ICFS)	n/a	Certified Future Strategists
UK	Oxford University	Department of Continuing Education	Certificate of Attendance for strategic planning and foresight: Learning from and managing for the future
UK	Oxford University	Saïd Business School	Oxford Scenarios Program
UK	University of Manchester	Manchester Institute of Innovation Research	The ART of Foresight & Sustainable Futures: Anticipating, Recommending and Transforming Research and Innovation Futures
USA	University of Houston	College of Technology	Professional Certificate in foresight

Source: Ross Dawson, *University futures and foresight degrees and programs*, accessed September 29, 2020, https://rossdawson.com/futurist/university-foresight-programs/

Note: The PhD program in organizational learning, performance, and change at my institution, Colorado State University, is not included here. For 10 years, we have offered a full-semester (three months) course dedicated to scenario planning that is open to anyone (degree enrollment is not required). As far as I am aware, it is the only full-semester course dedicated entirely to scenario planning. In it, we recruit companies and deliver scenario planning for them; students are arranged in groups and allocated to the companies we serve. While Dawson's efforts should be commended, it is probably impossible to put together an entirely comprehensive list.

References

Anderson, M. (1994). The rise and fall of strategic planning. *MIT Sloan Management Review, 35*(2), 107.

Asher, N., & Lascarides, A. (2013). Strategic conversation. *Semantics and Pragmatics, 6,* 2–11.

Austin, B. (1994). The rise and fall of strategic planning. *Academy of Management Perspectives, 8*(3), 19–24.

Baah, C., Jin, Z., & Tang, L. (2020). Organizational and regulatory stakeholder pressures friends or foes to green logistics practices and financial performance: Investigating corporate reputation as a missing link. *Journal of Cleaner Production, 247,* 119–125.

Benninga, S. (2014). *Financial modeling.* MIT Press.

Bodwell, W., & Chermack, T. J. (2010). Organizational ambidexterity: Integrating deliberate and emergent strategy with scenario planning. *Technological Forecasting and Social Change, 77*(2), 193–202.

Bohannan, P. (1995). *How culture works.* Free Press.

Brooks, B., & Curnin, S. (2021). Stretch-thinking loops: A new technique for scenario planning. *Risk, Hazards & Crisis in Public Policy, 12*(1), 110–124.

Caplan, R., & Boyd, D. (2018). Isomorphism through algorithms: Institutional dependencies in the case of Facebook. *Big Data & Society, 5*(1).

Capon, N. (1996). The rise and fall of strategic planning. *Academy of Management Review, 21*(1), 167–169.

Carter, T. R., La Rovere, E. L., Jones, R. N., Leemans, R., Mearns, L. O., Nakicenovic, N., ... & Skea, J. (2001). Developing and applying scenarios. In

Climate change 2001: Impacts, Adaptation, and Vulnerability, edited by James J. McCarthy, Osvaldo F. Canziani, Neil A. Leary, David J. Dokken, and Kasey S. White, 145–190. Cambridge University Press.

Chermack, T. J. (2004). Improving decision-making with scenario planning. *Futures, 36*(3), 295–309.

Chermack, T. J. (2011). *Scenario planning in organizations: How to create, use, and assess scenarios*. Berrett-Koehler.

Chermack, T. J. (2017). *Foundations of scenario planning: The story of Pierre Wack.* Routledge.

Chermack, T. J. (2018). An analysis and categorization of scenario planning scholarship from 1995–2016. *Journal of Futures Studies, 22*(4), 45–60.

Chermack, T. J. (2019). Response to Spaniol and Rowlands' *Defining Scenario* (Invited response—blind reviewed). *Futures & Foresight Science, 1*(2), 1–3.

Collingwood, H. (2001). The earnings game: Everyone plays, nobody wins. *Harvard Business Review, 79*(6), 65–74.

Cross, T., Prasad, R., & Ramlall, S. (2020, March 3). *Disruptive innovation goes to business school: Is the MBA dead?* The Evolllution. https://evolllution.com /programming/program_planning/disruptive-innovation-goes-to-business-school-is -the-mba-dead/

Dator, J., & Bezold, C. (Eds.). (1981). *Judging the future.* Wiley.

Davis, G. (2003). *Scenarios: An explorer's guide.* Shell Oil.

de Geus, A. P. (1992). Modelling to predict or to learn? *European Journal of Operational Research, 59*(1), 1–5.

de Ruijter, M. P. (2014). *Scenario based strategy: Navigate the future.* Ashgate Publishing, Ltd.

Deming, W. E. (1991). *W. Edwards Deming.* Madonna University.

Dredge, S. (2019, February 1). *Music created by artificial intelligence is better than you think.* OneZero. https://onezero.medium.com/music-created-by-artificial -intelligence-is-better-than-you-think-ce73631e2ec5

Elgammal, A. (2019). Advanced algorithms are using machine learning to create art autonomously. *American Scientist 107*(1), 18–19. https://www.americanscientist.org /article/ai-is-blurring-the-definition-of-artist

Emery, F. E., & Trist, E. L. (1965). The causal texture of organizational environments. *Human Relations, 18*(1), 21–32.

Favato, G., & Vecchiato, R. (2017). Embedding real options in scenario planning: A new methodological approach. *Technological Forecasting and Social Change, 124*, 135–149.

Fergnani, A., & Song, Z. (2020). The six scenario archetypes framework: A systematic investigation of science fiction films set in the future. *Futures, 124*(2), 102–125.

Foroohar, R. (2019). Why management by numbers doesn't add up. *Financial Times*. https://www.ft.com/content/2950e8ca-a489-11e9-a282-2df48f366f7d

Gelles, D., & Yaffe-Bellany, D. (2019, August 19). Shareholder value is no longer everything, top CEOs say. *The New York Times*, 1.

Gelsomino, L. M., de Boer, R., Steeman, M., & Perego, A. (2019). An optimisation strategy for concurrent supply chain finance schemes. *Journal of Purchasing and Supply Management, 25*(2), 185–196.

Godet, M. (2000). The art of scenarios and strategic planning: Tools and pitfalls. *Technological Forecasting and Social Change, 65*(1), 3–22.

Godet, M. (2001). *Creating futures*. Economica.

Goodwin, P. (2019). Scenarios and forecasts: Complementary ways of anticipating the future? *Foresight: The International Journal of Applied Forecasting*, (52), 7–10.

Gordon, A. V. (2020). Matrix purpose in scenario planning: Implications of congruence with scenario project purpose. *Futures, 115*, 102479.

Greiner, R., Puig, J., Huchery, C., Collier, N., & Garnett, S. T. (2014). Scenario modelling to support industry strategic planning and decision making. *Environmental Modelling & Software, 55*, 120–131.

Guerrera, F. (2009). Welch rues short-term profit 'obsession.' *Financial Times, 12*.

Hendry, J. (2002). The principal's other problems: Honest incompetence and the specification of objectives. *Academy of Management Review, 27*(1), 98–113.

Hines, A., & Bishop, P. C. (2013). Framework foresight: Exploring futures the Houston way. *Futures, 51*(1), 31–49.

Inayatullah, S. (1998). Causal layered analysis: Poststructuralism as method. *Futures, 30*(8), 815–829.

Inayatullah, S. (2002). Reductionism or layered complexity? The futures of futures studies. *Futures, 34*(3–4), 295–302.

Iyanda Ismail, A., Awawdeh, A., Al-Hiyari, A., & Isiaka Jimba, K. (2020). Moderating effects of management philosophy on high-performance work practices–firm performance relationship. *Journal of African Business*, 1–15.

Kahane, A. (1992). The Mont Fleur scenarios. *Deeper News, 7*(1), 1–22.

Kahane, A. (2004). *Solving tough problems: An open way of talking, listening, and creating new realities.* Berrett-Koehler Publishers.

Kahane, A. (2012). *Transformative scenario planning: Working together to change the future.* Berrett-Koehler Publishers.

Kanu, M. S. (2020). Integrating enterprise risk management with strategic planning for improved firm performance. *European Journal of Business and Management Research, 5*(5), 17–34.

Kaplan, R. S., & Norton, D. P. (2001). Transforming the balanced scorecard from performance measurement to strategic management: Part I. *Accounting Horizons, 15*(1), 87–104.

Konno, N., Nonaka, I., & Ogilvy, J. (2014). Scenario planning: The basics. *World Futures, 70*(1), 28–43.

Kono, P. M., & Barnes, B. (2010). The role of finance in the strategic-planning and decision-making process. *Graziadio Business Report, 13*(1), 1–17. https://gbr .pepperdine.edu/2010/08/the-role-of-finance-in-the-strategic-planning-and-decision -making-process/

Lew, C., Meyerowitz, D., & Svensson, G. (2019). Formal and informal scenario-planning in strategic decision-making: An assessment of corporate reasoning. *Journal of Business & Industrial Marketing, 34*(2), 439–450.

Lindgren, M., & Bandhold, H. (2003). *Scenario planning: The link between future and strategy.* Palgrave.

Long, W., Li, S., Wu, H., & Song, X. (2020). Corporate social responsibility and financial performance: The roles of government intervention and market competition. *Corporate Social Responsibility and Environmental Management, 27*(2), 525–541.

Manning, T. (2002). Strategic conversation as a tool for change. *Strategy & Leadership, 35*(5), 35–38.

Mattson, B. W. (2005). Using the critical outcome technique to demonstrate financial and organizational performance results. *Advances in Developing Human Resources, 7*(1), 102–120.

Meissner, P., Brands, C., & Wulf, T. (2017). Quantifying blind spots and weak signals in executive judgment: A structured integration of expert judgment into the scenario development process. *International Journal of Forecasting, 33*(1), 244–253.

Mendonça, S., Pina e Cunha, M., Kaivo-oja, J., & Ruff, F. (2004). Wild cards, weak signals and organisational improvisation. *Futures, 36*(2), 201–218.

Micklethwait, J., & Wooldridge, A. (1996). *The witch doctors: Making sense of the management gurus.* Crown Business.

Miles, I., & Popper, R. (2009). The many faces of foresight. In L. Georghiou, J. C. Harper, M. Keenan, I. Miles, & R. Popper (Eds.). *The handbook of technology foresight.* Edward Elgar Publishing Ltd.

Miles, L., & Poppe, H. (2017). When the finance department becomes a company's secret weapon. Bain & Company. Accessed June 17 2021 at https://www.bain.com/insights/when-the-finance-department-becomes-a-companys-secret-weapon-brief/.

Miller, C. C., & Cardinal, L. B. (1994). Strategic planning and firm performance: A synthesis of more than two decades of research. *Academy of Management Journal, 37*(6), 1649–1665.

Millon, D. (2002). Why is corporate management obsessed with quarterly earnings and what should be done about it. *George Washington Law Review, 70,* 890–898.

Mintzberg, H. (1994a). The fall and rise of strategic planning. *Harvard Business Review, 72*(1), 107–114.

Mintzberg, H. (1994b). Rethinking strategic planning part I: Pitfalls and fallacies. *Long Range Planning, 27*(3), 12–21.

Mintzberg, H. (2000). *The rise and fall of strategic planning.* Pearson Education.

Mintzberg, H. (2004). *Managers, not MBAs: A hard look at the soft practice of managing and management development.* Berrett-Koehler Publishers.

Mintzberg, H., Ahlstrand, B., & Lampel, J. B. (2020). *Strategy safari.* Pearson UK.

Mintzberg, H., & Lampel, J. (1999). Reflecting on the strategy process. *MIT Sloan Management Review, 40*(3), 21–25

Mintzberg, H., & Waters, J. A. (1985). Of strategies, deliberate and emergent. *Strategic Management Journal, 6*(3), 257–272.

Nalborczyk, L. (2020). Re-analysing the data from Moffatt et al. (2020): A textbook illustration of the absence of evidence fallacy, 1–26. https://psyarxiv.com/9j76v/

Nickell, S., & Nicolitsas, D. (1999). How does financial pressure affect firms? *European Economic Review, 43*(8), 1435–1456.

Nickols, F. (2016). Strategy, strategic management, strategic planning and strategic thinking. *Management Journal, 1*(1), 4–7.

Nilsson, F., Petri, C. J., & Westelius, A. (2020). *Strategic management control.* Springer.

Norris, M. (2019). Research methods in the psychological sciences. In In M. Norris (Ed.), *The Canadian handbook for careers in psychological science*, pp. 31–43. McGraw-Hill.

Obar, J. A. (2015). Big data and the phantom public: Walter Lippmann and the fallacy of data privacy self-management. *Big Data & Society, 2*(2), 2053951715608876.

Ocasio, W., & Joseph, J. (2008). Rise and fall—or transformation? The evolution of strategic planning at the General Electric Company, 1940–2006. *Long Range Planning, 41*(3), 248–272.

Ogilvy, J. A. (2002). *Creating better futures: Scenario planning as a tool for a better tomorrow.* Oxford University Press.

Ogilvy, J., & Schwartz, P. (2004). Plotting your scenarios. Global Business Network. Accessed May 17, 2021 at http://adaptknowledge.com/wp-content/uploads/rapidintake/PI_CL/media/gbn_Plotting_Scenarios.pdf.

Pearce, J. A., Freeman, E. B., & Robinson, R. B., Jr. (1987). The tenuous link between formal strategic planning and financial performance. *Academy of Management Review, 12*(4), 658–675.

Pignataro, P. (2013). *Financial modeling and valuation: A practical guide to investment banking and private equity* (Vol. 876). John Wiley & Sons.

Porter, M. E. (1980). *Competitive strategy.* Free Press.

Porter, M. E. (1985). *Competitive advantage.* Free Press.

Ralston, B., & Wilson, I. (2006). *The scenario planning handbook*: *A practitioner's guide to developing strategies in today's uncertain times* (pp. 18–20). Thomson South-Western, Mason.

Ramírez, R., & Selin, C. (2014). Plausibility and probability in scenario planning. *Foresight, 16*(1), 54–74.

Ramirez, R., & Wilkinson, A. (2014). Rethinking the 2 × 2 scenario method: Grid or frames? *Technological Forecasting and Social Change, 86*, 254–264.

Ramirez, R., & Wilkinson, A. (2016). *Strategic reframing: The Oxford scenario planning approach.* Oxford University Press.

Rein, M., & Schon, D. (1991). Framing in policy discourse. *Social Sciences and Modern States: National Experiences and Theoretical Crossroads, 9*, 262–279.

Rickards, L., Wiseman, J., Edwards, T., & Biggs, C. (2014). The problem of fit: Scenario planning and climate change adaptation in the public sector. *Environment and Planning C: Government and Policy, 32*(4), 641–662.

Rudd, J. M., Greenley, G. E., Beatson, A. T., & Lings, I. N. (2008). Strategic planning and performance: Extending the debate. *Journal of Business Research, 61*(2), 99–108.

Schaefer, T., & Guenther, T. (2016). Exploring strategic planning outcomes: The influential role of top versus middle management participation. *Journal of Management Control, 27*(2–3), 205–249.

Schein, E. H. (1985). Defining organizational culture. *Classics of Organization Theory, 3*(1), 490–502.

Schnaars, S. P. (1987). How to develop and use scenarios. *Long Range Planning, 20*(1), 105–114.

Schoemaker, P. J. (1993). Multiple scenario development: Its conceptual and behavioral foundation. *Strategic Management Journal, 14*(3), 193–213.

Schoemaker, P. J. (1995). Scenario planning: A tool for strategic thinking. *Sloan Management Review, 36*(2), 25–50.

Schoemaker, P. J. (2012). *Profiting from uncertainty: Strategies for succeeding no matter what the future brings.* Simon and Schuster.

Schoemaker, P. J. (2019). Attention and foresight in organizations. *Futures & Foresight Science, 1*(1), e5.

Schoemaker, P. J. (2020). How historical analysis can enrich scenario planning. *Futures & Foresight Science, 2*(3), 35–49.

Schoemaker, P. J., Day, G. S., & Snyder, S. A. (2013). Integrating organizational networks, weak signals, strategic radars and scenario planning. *Technological Forecasting and Social Change, 80*(4), 815–824.

Schwartz, P. (1996). *The art of the long view: Paths to strategic insight for yourself and your company.* Currency.

Schwartz, P. (2012). *The art of the long view: Planning for the future in an uncertain world.* Currency.

Servant-Miklos, V. F. (2019). The Harvard connection: How the case method spawned problem-based learning at McMaster University. *Health Professions Education, 5*(3), 163–171.

Silver, N. (2012). *The signal and the noise: Why so many predictions fail—but some don't.* Penguin.

Simpson, J. A., & Weiner, E. S. C. (1989). *Oxford English dictionary*. Clarendon Press.

Smith, J., Smith, R. L., Smith, R., & Bliss, R. (2011). *Entrepreneurial finance: Strategy, valuation, and deal structure*. Stanford University Press.

Spaniol, M. J., & Rowland, N. J. (2018). The scenario planning paradox. *Futures, 95*, 33–43.

Swanson, R. A. (2001). *Assessing the financial benefits of human resource development*. Basic Books.

Swanson, R. A., Holton, E. F., & Holton, E. (1999). *Results: How to assess performance, learning, and perceptions in organizations*. Berrett-Koehler Publishers.

Teasdale, S. (2002). Culture eats strategy for breakfast! *Journal of Innovation in Health Informatics, 10*(4), 195–196.

Toney, F., & Brown, S. (1997). The incompetent CEO. *Journal of Leadership Studies, 4*(3), 84–98.

van der Heijden, K. (1996). *Scenarios: The art of strategic conversation*. John Wiley & Sons.

van der Heijden, K. (2004). Can internally generated futures accelerate organizational learning? *Futures, 36*(2), 145–159.

van der Heijden, K. (2005). *Scenarios: The art of strategic conversation* (2nd ed.). John Wiley & Sons.

van der Heijden, K. (2011). *Scenarios: The art of strategic conversation* (3rd ed.). John Wiley & Sons.

Varum, C. A., & Melo, C. (2010). Directions in scenario planning literature—A review of the past decades. *Futures, 42*(4), 355–369.

Wack, P. (1984). Scenarios designed to improve decision making. *Planning Review, 2*(2), 24–36.

Wack, P. (1985a). Scenarios: Shooting the rapids. *Harvard Business Review, 63*(6): 139–150.

Wack, P. (1985b). *Scenarios: The gentle art of re-perceiving*. Unpublished manuscript, Harvard Business School.

Wack, P. (1985c). Scenarios: Uncharted waters ahead. *Harvard Business Review, 63*(5): 73–89.

Wade, W. (2012). *Scenario planning: A field guide to the future*. John Wiley & Sons.

Warren, K. (2012). *The trouble with strategy*. Strategy Dynamics.

Whitzman, C. (2016). "Culture eats strategy for breakfast": The powers and limitations of urban design education. *Journal of Urban Design, 21*(5), 574–576.

Wilkinson, A., & Kupers, R. (2013). Living in the futures. *Harvard Business Review, 91*(5), 118–127.

Wilkinson, A., & Kupers, R. (2014). *The essence of scenarios.* Amsterdam University Press.

Wolf, C., & Floyd, S. W. (2017). Strategic planning research: Toward a theory-driven agenda. *Journal of Management, 43*(6), 1754–1788.

Wollenberg, E., Edmunds, D., & Buck, L. (2000). Using scenarios to make decisions about the future: Anticipatory learning for the adaptive co-management of community forests. *Landscape and Urban Planning, 47*(1–2), 65–77.

Wright, G., & Goodwin, P. (1999). Future-focussed thinking: Combining scenario planning with decision analysis. *Journal of Multi-Criteria Decision Analysis, 8*(6), 311–321.

Wright, M., Filatotchev, I., Hoskisson, R. E., & Peng, M. W. (2005). Strategy research in emerging economies: Challenging the conventional wisdom. *Journal of Management Studies, 42*(1), 1–33.

Zeleny, M. (1997). The fall of strategic planning. *Human Systems Management, 16*(2), 77.

Zhang, Y., & Gimeno, J. (2016). Earnings pressure and long-term corporate governance: Can long-term-oriented investors and managers reduce the quarterly earnings obsession? *Organization Science, 27*(2), 354–372.

Acknowledgments

Many people and organizations have contributed to the research, development, and practice that ultimately led to the writing of this book. In the early years, the focus was on understanding what makes for useful scenarios, and it quickly became clear that creating scenarios was very different from learning how to use them to achieve organizational change. Organizations that have provided support for developing the ideas in this book include Abbott Laboratories, Anglo American Corporation, Ferrellgas, Mitsubishi Chemical, World Academy of Sport, Lockheed Martin, Monsanto, Honeywell International, Boeing, Microsoft, RK Mechanical, Cargill, the City of Littleton, and Centura Health, among many others.

Important contributions to the processes, workshops, and intellectual and practical utility of *Using Scenarios* have come from Laura Coons, Justin Allen, Madison Murphy, Tamria Zertuche, Lauren Lambert, Felix Weitzman, TK Stoudt, Sarah Acer, Jerome Dixon, Gretchen Gagel, Kevin Lindsey, Scott Freshwater, Zach Mercurio, Cynthia Selin, Alessandro Fergnani, Delaney Keating, David Fincham, John Vann, Tiffany Yates, Mike Manfredo, and many, many others.

I am particularly grateful to Richard A. Swanson, a mentor and friend for over 20 years. The instruction and guidance I have received from him have been essential to my career and to my life. Steve Piersanti at Berrett-Koehler shepherded my first book back in 2011, and the lessons he taught have been mainstays of my approach to writing. Thank you to Charlotte Ashlock, who has managed this project with elegance. It has been a pleasure to work with you. Finally, thank you to Colorado State University for the support and freedom to pursue my interests and passions over the past 15 years.

It would be impossible to thank everyone with whom I had interactions that led to the outcomes contained in this book. More people and organizations than I can recognize here have supported this work, and I sincerely thank them all.

Page numbers in italics indicate figures.

Thomas J. Chermack is a professor of organizational learning, performance, and change
at Colorado State University, where he also
directs the Scenario Planning Institute. He has
served as the PhD program chair for 15 years.
He is also the founder and president of Chermack Scenarios (www.chermackscenarios.com),
a scenario planning consultancy firm. As a
researcher, he has focused on studying the
history and outcomes of scenario planning, as
well as the theoretical, practical, and academic

utility of scenario planning. He is the author of *Scenario Planning in Organizations*, *Foundations of Scenario Planning: The Story of Pierre Wack*, and
Theory Building in Applied Disciplines, which are considered foundational contributions to the field. Chermack has focused on how organizational leaders
use scenarios to manage uncertainty, and he is often quoted in academic
research and consults widely in regard to scenarios. He is also a frequent
speaker at planning and futures conferences around the world.

Berrett–Koehler
Publishers

Berrett-Koehler is an independent publisher dedicated to an ambitious mission: *Connecting people and ideas to create a world that works for all.*

Our publications span many formats, including print, digital, audio, and video. We also offer online resources, training, and gatherings. And we will continue expanding our products and services to advance our mission.

We believe that the solutions to the world's problems will come from all of us, working at all levels: in our society, in our organizations, and in our own lives. Our publications and resources offer pathways to creating a more just, equitable, and sustainable society. They help people make their organizations more humane, democratic, diverse, and effective (and we don't think there's any contradiction there). And they guide people in creating positive change in their own lives and aligning their personal practices with their aspirations for a better world.

And we strive to practice what we preach through what we call "The BK Way." At the core of this approach is *stewardship,* a deep sense of responsibility to administer the company for the benefit of all of our stakeholder groups, including authors, customers, employees, investors, service providers, sales partners, and the communities and environment around us. Everything we do is built around stewardship and our other core values of *quality, partnership, inclusion,* and *sustainability.*

This is why Berrett-Koehler is the first book publishing company to be both a B Corporation (a rigorous certification) and a benefit corporation (a for-profit legal status), which together require us to adhere to the highest standards for corporate, social, and environmental performance. And it is why we have instituted many pioneering practices (which you can learn about at www.bkconnection.com), including the Berrett-Koehler Constitution, the Bill of Rights and Responsibilities for BK Authors, and our unique Author Days.

We are grateful to our readers, authors, and other friends who are supporting our mission. We ask you to share with us examples of how BK publications and resources are making a difference in your lives, organizations, and communities at www.bkconnection.com/impact.

Dear reader,

Thank you for picking up this book and welcome to the worldwide BK community! You're joining a special group of people who have come together to create positive change in their lives, organizations, and communities.

What's BK all about?

Our mission is to connect people and ideas to create a world that works for all.

Why? Our communities, organizations, and lives get bogged down by old paradigms of self-interest, exclusion, hierarchy, and privilege. But we believe that can change. That's why we seek the leading experts on these challenges—and share their actionable ideas with you.

A welcome gift

To help you get started, we'd like to offer you a **free copy** of one of our bestselling ebooks:

www.bkconnection.com/welcome

When you claim your **free ebook**, you'll also be subscribed to our blog.

Our freshest insights

Access the best new tools and ideas for leaders at all levels on our blog at ideas.bkconnection.com.

Sincerely,

Your friends at Berrett-Koehler

Certified

Corporation